THE BALEARICS

THE BALEARICS

Islands of Enchantment

BY

JEAN-LOUIS COLAS BRD

TRANSLATED BY CHRISTINE TROLLOPE

RAND McNALLY & COMPANY

Rand McNally & Company edition published in the United States
and possessions in 1967

Library of Congress Catalog Card Number : 67—11465

PRINTED IN GREAT BRITAIN

Contents

MAPS

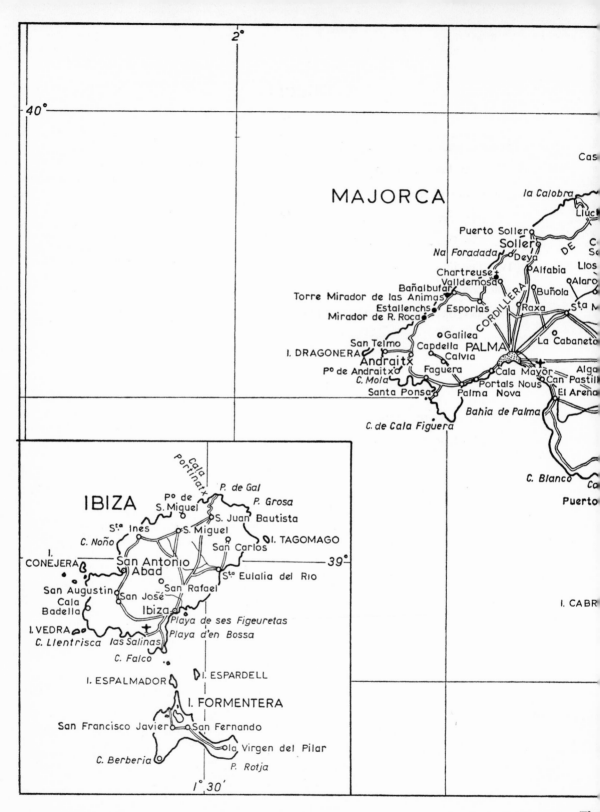

1. *The*

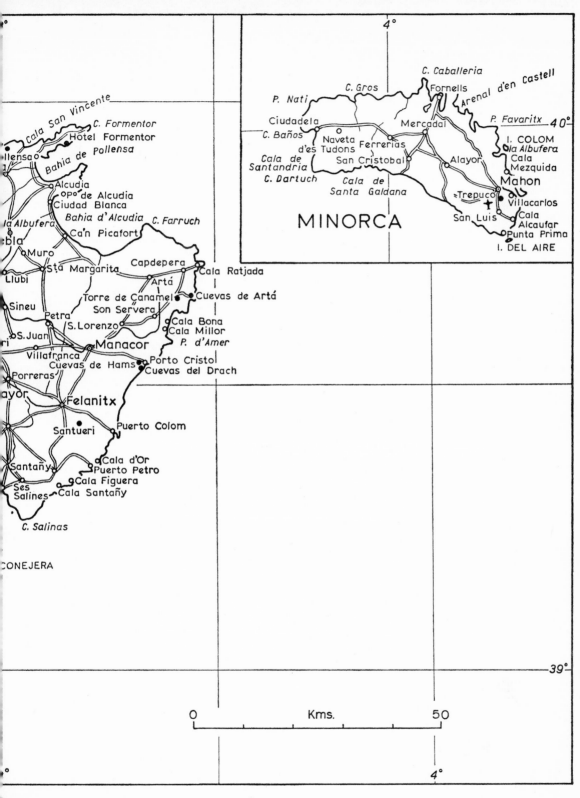

Cala San Vincente
C. Formentor
Hotel Formentor
llensao
Bahia de Pollensa
Alcudia
o p° de Alcudia
Ciudad Blanca
Bahia d'Alcudia
C. Farruch
Ca'n Picafort
la Albufera
bla
Muro
Capdepera
Cala Ratjada
Stª Margarita
Llubi
Artá
Cuevas de Artá
Sineu
Torre de Canamel
Son Servera
Petra
S. Lorenzo
Cala Bona
Cala Millor
P. d'Amer
S. Juan
Manacor
ri
Villafranca
Porto Cristo
Cuevas de Hams
Porreras
Cuevas del Drach
ayor
Felanitx
Santueri
Puerto Colom
Santañy
Cala d'Or
Puerto Petro
Ses
Salines
Cala Figuera
Cala Santañy
C. Salinas

CONEJERA

MINORCA

4°
C. Caballeria
Fornells
Arenal d'en Castell
C. Gros
P. Nati
Mercadal
P. Favaritx 40°
Ciudadela
I. COLOM
C. Baños
Naveta
d'es Tudons
Ferrerias
la Albufera
Cala de
Santandria
San Cristobal
Alayor
Cala
Mezquida
C. Dartuch
Cala de
Santa Galdana
Mahon
Trepuco
Villacarlos
San Luis
Cala
Alcaufar
Punta Prima
I. DEL AIRE

0   Kms.   50

39°

4°

lands.

Introduction

THE MAGIC MOUNTAIN

THE mountain of Formentor. . . . I see it from my window, every morning as I wake. Why, after three years of loving the island so deeply and exploring is so well, is it this mountain which suddenly seems to hold the key to the mystery, to be entrusted with the task of teaching me to know Majorca as I should?

Perched on its height, like a fez on a Moslem's head, is the *atalaya* or watch-tower, from which the watchman looked unceasingly out over every horizon, and gave warning of the slightest danger by blowing a conch which could be heard through all the region. At once peasants and fishermen withdrew into their fortified towns, leaving their boats and their crops and carrying to safety the most precious of their belongings. Alas! there was not always time. Too often pirates, acting with the speed and precision of lightning, either by a sudden sortie or after a fierce battle, would carry off boys and maidens to be sold in the slave markets of Africa. Majorca lived with this suffering for centuries; and today on every summit the *atalaya* reminds us of those barbarous days. It is a sight we cannot avoid; wherever we look it lends to the landscape its characteristic outline.

I look down a little, and my gaze lingers among the paths which cross and recross the hillside. Are they all true footpaths? After a few moments it is hard to distinguish between the deliberately man-made and those sketched in by chance, perhaps even by an optical illusion, a strange subtle hallucination leading the eye up and down, backwards and forwards in pursuit of random lines of objects. It takes so little to give an illusion of a path. If two juniper bushes seem for an instant to follow in line – there it is, winding between them! And then it is lost in a thorny tangle. We see it again almost at once and decide that it is really there, still going in the same direction. But meanwhile other paths have insidiously appeared, and we follow them, and no longer know which continues which. And so after a few minutes the whole mountain is caught as it were in a network of paths, each more obscure, more useless, than the last—since no one, neither man nor goat, ever follows them. And yet, for that very reason, they are so lovely, so evocative! Just as the sea forms its lines of billows, so this mountain creates waves of greenery and lacy crests of rock. . . . There it is before my eyes, massive and imponderable, hung from the sky like an arras. And it is as a tapestry that I see it – a tapestry hanging on my bedroom

11

wall, its every motif constantly changing in the shifting pattern of half-sleep, so that, watching it, one can go on dreaming for ever. . . .

Wandering up and down these mountain paths in the early morning, I have often lost myself completely among them. I am bewildered by their fragrant mazes. What strange ideas haunt me, soothe me, enchant me? I smell the wild sharp fragrance of the shrubs, and pass my hand over the rough warm surface of these everlasting rocks. . . . But are they everlasting? If we photographed them in ten years' time, would we find their white and grey skeletons, the green or scorched grass that covers them, all in the same place as before? And yet how many centuries it must have taken to give them this pearly hue or these indefinable shades of purple! . . . Suns have risen and set, and they have remained immovable. Can it be that they represent but an instant in the infinite history of nature, that hidden forces are even now undermining them, secretly preparing the whole island for a cataclysm corresponding to that which must once have thrust it up from the depths of the sea in a jet of molten granite? How can we believe such a thing, on this shining morning when every moment sheds its own happiness, spreading through the universe in an ecstasy that cannot but be eternal? What, then, is immortal, and where does dissolution begin?

Photographs only deceive. Then why not fingerprints? The mountain offering its great thumb to some official. . . . What nonsense! Truth lies in this perpetual motion, this constant changing; and it is strange that it should be, of all things, a *mountain* that appears to me to shift like a wave or a cloud. Yet how splendid it is in its terrible barrenness, bearing on its harsh breast a few tufts of greenery for the sun to paint in beauty. Only the pine clings to the lower slopes, invincibly, but its advance goes neither far nor high. All too soon it meets the naked rock, which allows no seed to settle, but offers its proud forehead to the kiss of the wind, while the rain washes its cheek like marble. Is that why I love it so, this mountain – because, in this land of fertility and easy happiness, it represents all that is useless, untouchable, untameable? It has no dealings with anything or anyone but heaven. It deigns to be beautiful in the daytime, when the sun plays at making mirages of every kind on its surface; but when night falls it becomes without regret a shadowy, almost invisible shape, wrapped in its loneliness, a black mass above a dark sea.

And now the sun as it moves is changing the view imperceptibly. . . . A shifting of the shadows, a slight movement of my head on the pillow, are enough. The mountain is lonely no longer; its head is crowned with clouds, its base fringed with foam. And there at last is the beach, the *playa transparente*, on which I constantly imagine I see the hero of *Les Ombres blanches* at the moment when he falls mortally wounded on the dazzling white sand. . . . Why should it be Polynesia that spring to my mind?

Strange as it may seem, I cannot help it. I remember my first sight of Formentor. I had already glimpsed in the distance the extraordinary hotel which had just been built there, in defiance of all the dictates of prudence, by the paradoxical whim of a poet seeking to bring life into the wilderness – it has since met with extraordinary success, and I am staying there now – but I did not know the beach. I was on my way from Pollensa and had just rounded the lighthouse point, when I suddenly saw, fringing the incredibly limpid blue of the sea, this pure white sand, gleaming like pearl dust and outlined by green pine-trees. It was all so fresh, so new, like another Eden. There was not a soul in sight. Only the white *casita*, long and low, seemed to call up images of a peaceful colonial existence. Why should a landscape, suddenly glimpsed, make me think of another I have never seen but which has been intensely vivid in my dreams? That is one of the mysteries of human life, which is a fabric woven of a thousand threads of past and future, with all the wavering random patterns of memory and pre-sentiment, of certainty and illusion. But I know that when I first saw this spot, as the boat neared the shore, I cried out in spite of myself: "Oceania!" And I remembered all the stories which ancient mariners have told of an earthly Paradise far different from our sombre clime. Formentor. . . . I had never seen a lovelier shore in the whole of the Mediterranean; nor have I since.

I bathed there every morning for weeks. I gathered coral there. I let its twilight steal upon me as I lay in unending meditation on one subject and one only – that bay, so perfectly formed that it reminds me of those Greek or Sicilian shores which seem to be born not of a freak of geology but the inspiration of an artist-god. I love it as I would a living being, and in the same way I dread that it may be corrupted by change.

I seem to hear the unchanging mountain reply that it at least can expect a kind of immortality. It was there, myrtles, carob-trees, pines and all, before the Moors, before the Romans, and before the Phoenicians. It was there even before the beach, formed by the sea over centuries spent patiently grinding precious fragments of marble, granite and coral. . . . And as it stands rejoicing in its pride, I seem to see it quiver gently, like a curtain about to rise on the gorgeous spectacle of the island.

FRANCIS DE MIOMANDRE

Chapter I

ISLAND DESTINY

IF we were to draw up a kind of inventory of the expressions applied over the centuries to the Balearic Islands, these epithets, often bestowed as official names, would be enough to give us an idea of the essential character of the islands. The etymology of the term *Balearic* is doubtful; some consider it a word of Phoenician origin from the name of the sun-god Baal, while others derive it from the Greek word *ballein* (to hurl) referring to the traditional accomplishment of the inhabitants, who, long before the days of Sallust, were the Balearic slingers of legend. Strabo called them the 'Happy Isles' (Eudaemones). Certain Christian writers, such as Saint Jerome and Saint Isidore, refer to them only as 'insulae Aphrodisiacae' (the reference is probably a purely literary one to the islanders' cult of the Goddess of Beauty). It was the Romans who finally gave them their name: Balearis Major (the larger) which became Majorca, and Balearis Minor (the smaller) which became Minorca. The seventeenth-century historian Dameto[1] mentions two names given in ancient times to Majorca and Minorca: one was called Clumba and the other Nura. In support of his theory he calmly informs us that Clumba comes from the Latin *Columba* by the omission of the 'o', and that the ancient name C(o)lumba thus refers to the well-known spot in Majorca called the Palomera. . . .

The word Pithyuses, which Strabo uses to designate Ibiza and Formentera, has an equally uncertain etymology; it probably refers to the pine forests which covered these two island before the mass deforestation carried out by the islanders. The suffix -*ussus* is said to be a survival of a Phoenician word-ending once applied to all the islands in the archipelago.[2]

The words change a little, but on the whole the Balearic Islands remain simply and unpretentiously named throughout the centuries. It is not until the nineteenth century – and to an even greater degree the present day – that they take on as many names as a chameleon has colours. They are the 'Isles of Enchantment', the 'Island of Light', the 'Mecca of Painters', the 'Islands of the Sun'. Majorca, in particular, becomes (for Rusiñol) the 'Tranquil Isle'; George Sand called it 'green Helvetia beneath a Calabrian sky, with the solemnity and silence

---

[1] Juan Dameto, *La Historia General del reigno Balearico*. English translation, London 1716.
[2] See footnote 3 on page 33.

of the East'. Behind these names, incomplete as they all are, lurks the unchanging reality of landscape and atmosphere.

Every year almost two million travellers leave for the islands by sea or air. Palma is no longer a mysterious city clinging to the shores of a remote bay; endowed as it is with two long piers and an airport which can take jets, it is the focal point of the densest stream of tourist in western Europe. It is sought alike by the wealthiest and by those of humbler means, and is developing to an extent found in few other places in the world. The mills of Es Jonquet, embedded like fossils in the centre of the town, bear witness to a past when Palma was no more than a cluster of buildings tightly enclosed within its walls. At the beginning of the twentieth century the demolition of the walls began, exposing the peripheral road which begins at the Avenida General Primo de Rivera and joins the sea-front at the Paseo Mallorca. Under the intense pressure of the population expansion – largely due to the tourist industry – the capital of the Balearic Islands has nowadays become a vast building site. The old town clustered round the Borne and the cathedral remains intact, with its streets, its *patios*, and its wonderful memories. The transformation is taking place in the border areas between the residential districts where hotels were first built, and the quarters where the working population used to live. The houses of Es Jonquet are surviving examples of the type of building which has been demolished. This site has been preserved on account of the picturesque appearance of the mills, but the whole of the neighbouring quarter is to be pulled down to make way for large groups of modern buildings.

The little town with its narrow streets and dusty avenues is no longer to be seen. The traditional setting of the capital of the Balearic Islands is gradually giving place to landscaped promenades and luxury hotels ('air conditioned throughout' as the advertisements say). It is a playground for the illustrious, a paradise for royal honeymoons. And on those same quays where the great ships come in, there move other figures, drawn there by the prospect of escape from their island life: dockers, porters, taxi-drivers, couriers from the tourist agencies, each with headgear more martial than the next; all those to whom the daily routine of the port is no picturesque dream but a series of tasks revolving mainly round the satisfaction of all the many demands of the tourist coming to spend a few days in Palma, in Majorca, in the islands. In their eyes the newcomer is rich, and comes, rather like the Brazilian in *La Vie Parisienne*, to spend money for his own pleasure; these people welcoming him were born in a village or town on one of the islands, living sometimes in one room overcrowded with brothers and sisters; they are aristocrats fallen on bad days, or astute men of business, or touts, often from humble families. They do not come to beg, but their entire income is from their business exchanges with the newly-arrived tourist. Less than ten years ago the way of life of most of the islanders was much nearer to that of the grand-parents of most of the visitors: self-absorbed, self-supporting communities where time flowed steadily past. Then everything happened at

once, and in a few years the simple Mediterranean peasant villages became play-grounds as sophisticated as California or Florida. And yet the good old days (which were not so good after all) and sometimes even the Middle Ages or the days of antiquity, are things of only yesterday.

We might perhaps be tempted to try to explain why two so different ways of life should be found side by side. We might, like the highly coloured leaflets of the tourist agencies, speak of the incomparable beauty of the Bay of Palma, the mildness of the climate, the hospitality of the natives, the cheapness of hotels, and the comparatively easy life.

But the whole secret of the success of the Balearic Islands lies in the fact that they are islands. Islands, great or small, are always a source of wonder to man : their reputation goes far beyond their dimensions, which are often modest. There is nothing commonplace about them. Some have suffered a dreadful fate and become convict settlements, scrap-heaps of humanity : Poulo Condore, Saint-Laurent de Cayenne, Makronissos, and, very recently, New Caledonia. Others have sheltered bloody murderers; still others have been the homes of pirates, lovers of gold and of liberty : Ulysses of Ithaca, Blackbeard of Turtle Island, Misson of the Mascarene Islands. Some have been havens of peace and refuge for the persecuted; some, like Easter Island, baffle us with their gigantic statues; and some, like Malta, Cyprus and the Falkland Islands are or have been military bases.

But the destiny of islands has always been extraordinary, and the Balearic Islands are no exception.

They are five in number : Minorca, Majorca, Ibiza, Formentera and Cabrera. They lie in the western part of the Mediterranean where ships have sailed since the remotest days of antiquity, and though they are not large as islands go, they form nevertheless 'a consistent whole both racially and historically, in so far as they have been affected by influences making them, at one and the same time, very advanced and very backward in relation to the history of the sea in general; they have always been torn between the two extremes of the old and the new'.[1] For example, as far as Ibiza is concerned, its very small size and its particular type of physical features have allowed it, until a few years ago, to exist as a self-contained unit, with its own language, its own customs, its own outdated methods of agriculture, and even its own fauna (such as green lizards, and dogs claimed to be descended from a Phoenician breed). Its peasants speak a peculiar dialect called *Ibicenco*, which a Castilian would find hard to understand. Its rustic dwellings are built in a style all their own, and its women wear a severe type of costume rather like that of the Ile de Sein, in Brittany. This involuntary withdrawal has led to the preservation up to the present day of traditional costumes which are of particular interest to tourists. In contrast to this self-absorption we may note that when the island does, from time to time, make contact with the outside

[1] F. Braudel, *La Méditerranée au temps de Philippe II*. Armand-Colin, 1949

world, it happens suddenly and spasmodically. 'Then all at once, with some chance reversal of fortune or change of master, it acquires a new set of customs, a new life, a new civilisation.'[1] This leads to a strange kind of stratification, built up of the civilizations brought by Phoenicians, Carthaginians, Greeks, Lydians, Phocaeans, Romans and the Latinized colonists of Iberia, Goths and Vandals, Arabs and Berbers, Genoese, Pisans, Aragonese and Catalans. The 'isolation' of an island cannot last for ever.

It has often been said that an island awakens each time it overcomes the precarious nature of its means of existence.

The tourist, especially if he comes from the north, should by the time he reaches the Balearic Islands 'have shed a certain number of prejudices. Coming from a dark, fog-bound country, he is dazzled by the sun, the colours, the warm air, the almond blossom, the early fruit. He sees everything in a glow of light and joy and easy gaiety, and he is apt to assume all too easily that all this is bestowed and never striven for. He is bewildered by it, and incomprehension and ill-will combine to make him too quick to talk about laziness.'[2] How blind he is to the basic harshness of these poetic isles! Nature, here, however seductive she may seem, has had to be conquered. And victory comes only after a twofold struggle; first of all certain unfavourable physical conditions have had to be overcome, such as soil insufficient in depth and unprotected from the effects of wind and water. After that the changing seasons have to be watched, and sowing, harvesting and getting in carried on according to a very strict time-table.

Beginning with spring, that enchanted season when the blossom hangs on the almond, orange, lemon, mandarin, peach and apricot trees, life on the farms becomes more and more hectic. The corn is harvested in May or June, figs in August, grapes in September, olives in October, and ploughing begins with the first autumn rains.

Even that is nothing to what happens in the towns as soon as the season begins. Floods of tourists arrive and have to be housed, catered for, and amused. Thus the inhabitants of the Balearic Islands whether they live in town or country, are permanently under the necessity of acting quickly. They can never put off their work until *mañana*, tomorrow. They must all of them earn in six months enough to live for the whole year.

Islands have only one way of escaping from their loneliness; they can turn outwards and become a link in a chain, a useful part of some system of exchanges, whatever it may be. In modern times salvation has come first of all from emigration. The finest export of the Balearic Islands is men. They send their sons to New York and South America, and even more to France (and until recently to Algeria), where they carry on a wide variety of trades thanks to their easy adaptability and the intelligence common to all Mediterranean races. Farmers

[1] *ibid.*   [2] *ibid.*

from Mahon have gone to Orania, and people from the islands man the stalls of early vegetables and exotic fruit which lend light and colour to the quiet streets of French provincial towns. But not all the islanders emigrate. Those who remain are anxious to raise their standard of living. They develop their vine-yards, their maize-fields or their olive-groves, but most of all they seek to increase tourism by a rapid expansion of the hotel industry, and thus, while attempting to tap the hard currencies of the world – sterling, dollars and francs – they play their part in the awakening of the islands.

Ortega y Gasset defined the Spaniard as 'the man of the *plaza mayor*', that open space, which custom insists should be rectangular, found in all towns in Spain and Latin America. In the Balearic Islands, impregnated above all with Catalon civilisation, things are rather different. The islander, like the Catalan, is no less the man of the *plaza mayor*, though his venue is the *ramblas*, the plane-bordered avenues which come to life at dusk. The setting is not the *plaza mayor*, but the motives inspiring the strollers are the same; the thing is to be seen there. It is a thoroughly Mediterranean trait, found in Beirut, in Athens, in Istanbul, in the Piazza San-Marco in Venice, and in Algiers, in what was once the Place du Gouvernement. In Palma everyone, dressed in his best, meets his friends in the Borne, the Paseo de Generalisimo Franco. They stroll in the plane-tree shade at about one o'clock – aperitif time – and at seven in the evening. Soldiers wear their dress uniforms; girls, walking two by two, make personal remarks accompanied by giggles; tourists come in search of what they imagine to be local colour, but see only the outside, the façade as it were, of the Majorcan people. The Majorcans enter into the spirit of things willingly enough, but without illusions. They know they exist for other people's benefit, that they are being watched. There too the fact that they are islanders determines their nature; there is this continual need to define themselves in relation to something outside themselves.

Nowadays the sea brings the tourists. But for a long time it was the only means of existence unless one depended entirely on the soil. At one time Palma was at the head of a regular Catalan thalassocracy. When at the end of the thirteenth century king Jaime divided his kingdom between his two sons, Majorca and the Balearic Islands took their place in history. Jaime II received Majorca, Roussillon, the Cerdagne valley and the Seigniory of Montpellier. Palma then became the capital of an ill-assorted group of territories, and prepared to reach the zenith of its glory and that of the islands. At that period the world envied the Majorcans, who dressed like lords. They appeared everywhere, on the land routes from Barcelona to Montpellier via Perpignan; they traded with Genoa, bringing wool from the Iberian peninsula and salt from Ibiza, and buying linen; certain families had the monopoly of trade in alum. This was the period when they began to travel long distances from home. Some went as far as the Atlantic. From 1281 onwards they were to be found in London, and they were among the first Mediterraneans to return to England, at the same time as the

Genoese. They established themselves as the carriers of the Mediterranean, parsimoniously handing out the salt they sold to the Genoese; their glazed pottery, majolica ware, was to serve as models for the Italian potters of the Renaissance.

This commercial and political flowering at the height of the mediaeval period was balanced by a brilliant intellectual radiance; Ramon Llull won for himself a place in the forefront of the history of ideas.

He was born in 1235 of a well-to-do family like that of St Francis of Assisi, Pascal and Père de Foucauld, and began by leading an adventurous life in Navarre, Castille and Montpellier. He then became a page at the court of James I and even tutor to his son James II. These were years of dissipation and amorous adventures no different from those of any other young libertine. However, in 1257 he married Blanca Picany who bore him two children. According to the legend as related by Brantôme, Don Ramon Llull loved to desperation Doña Ambrosia de Castello, the most virtuous and most beautiful woman in Palma, and followed her everywhere she went. One day he even went so far as to follow her on horseback into a church. Faced with such a scandal, the virtuous wife went to her husband for advice, and he left it to her to choose the best method of discouraging her suitor. Doña Ambrosia, in a last meeting with Ramon Llull, unfastened her gown and laid bare her breast covered with cancerous tumours. 'Look,' she said, 'such is earthly beauty; only the beauty of divine love can last.'

After this shattering scene, Ramon Llull's life took a completely different turn. In fact his conversion took place on a hot summer night in 1265, in circumstances slightly reminiscent of Pascal's 'Night of fire'. He made pilgrimages to Rocamadour, Saint James of Compostella, and Montserrat, and returned to Majorca. He then realized his vocation as missionary to the Jews and Moslems. He wrote an 'art of thinking' to demonstrate the Truth he aspired to teach, and worked out for that purpose a veritable technique of conversion. In order to convert, one must at least be able to speak the language of the country visited; so Ramon Llull studied Arabic and Hebrew.

In 1276 he founded Miramar. He dreamed of teaching languages, so founded the first school of Oriental languages. His aim was to train missionary interpreters. Then he left Majorca and for the next few years wandered about the world.

We see him first in Paris, and then he may have made a complete tour around the Mediterranean. Passing through Byzantium, he is said to have gone as far as Georgia. Some claim to have found traces of him in Egypt, perhaps even in Ethiopia and as far south as the Sudan. He returned to Rome at the time of the Sicilian Vespers, by way of Cyrenaica, Ceuta, Granada and Almeria. During this period he worked at the perfecting of his 'art of conversion' according to a sort of 'pre-Jesuit' technique. He taught at the Sorbonne and at Montpellier. He returned to Genoa, then to Rome, where he tried to interest Nicholas IV in a plan for the conquest of the Holy Land. After that he worked alone at the immense and inspired task of converting the infidel. After the incident at Bougie when he was almost stoned, he was expelled from Africa and sailed to Pisa where he was shipwrecked.

He remained for two years in Italy; in 1269 at Assisi where he was attending a meeting of Minorite brothers, he tried to persuade Philip the Fair, king of France, to lauch another crusade. For thirteen years he divided his time between visits to his native island and voyages to distant parts.

In 1313 a peace treaty was signed between the king of Majorca and the rulers of Tunis; the bonds between the two powers were strengthened particularly by the existence of banks or *fondjouks* run by Majorcans on Islam territory. Ramon Llull set out once again to convert the Moors. He left Tunis in December 1315. Legend has it that he was stoned to death for his preaching and missionary activities, but in fact he almost certainly died in his native island after a long illness.[1] 'I have abandoned wife, children and worldly goods and have spent thirty years in torment and suffering.'[2] And that in fact sums up the extraordinary life of Ramon Llull.

It is a remarkable fact that this muscular Christian, at once intellectual and man action, this 'globe-trotter of the faith', led a life to all outward appearances the same as that of the merchant-princes of Palma who sailed over all the Mediterranean; and thus he provides a striking illustration of the part played by the Balearic Islands in bringing together the whole Mediterranean into one unit. They were cosmopolitan even in the Middle Ages.

A little later we see the arrival of the nomadic element par excellence in the Jews who came from the Maghrib and Macedonia. In the fourteenth century they were the best cartographers of their time apart from the Genoese. The *portolani* of Palma were used by navigators until the new Atlantic routes were opened.

After this golden age when they played an exceptional part in international politics, the Balearic Islands entered upon a more tranquil era. The age of great discoveries caused a torpor to fall upon the Mediterranean, and the islands withdrew into themselves, leaving the monopoly of the gold trade to Seville; the era of busy commercial capitalism was followed by one of relative inactivity. The Balearic Islands no longer played an active part in history, but became a pawn in the game. The French and the English were fighting over Minorca in the eighteenth century, but at that time islands could do no more than submit, and with so precarious a future their usefulness as refuges was over. From then onwards the Balearic Islands produced only isolated men of genius: Father Serra, the last of the Conquistadors, who discovered California, the surgeon Orfila and the admiral Farragut. . . . It was not until the nineteenth century that they were rediscovered, thanks to Chopin's diseased lungs. Then they became the

[1] A. Llinares, 'Le dramatique épisode algérien de la vie de Ramon Llull'. *Revue de la Méditerranée*, 1959.

[2] *Lo Desconhort*, stanza XIV, lines 159-160 (written in 1295).

lonely shores to which the intrepid holiday-makers of France could make their voyages of discovery.

This withdrawal kept the Balearic Islands out of the great European cataclysms. The Spanish Civil War of 1936 did not shake them deeply. There were of course fierce battles there as there were everywhere; but the cathedral of Palma was not destroyed, nor the citadel of Ibiza, nor the mills of Formentera, nor the *talayots* of Minorca; they are all still there for the tourist to see.

The destiny of the islands is a strange paradox. In the thirteenth century they were in advance of the world; five centuries before Champollion, Ramon Llull had the first inklings of Egyptology, learned to speak Oriental languages and developed his powers of reasoning; the merchants of Palma captured the world's markets ahead of the Genoese. We might almost say they were modern before modernity existed. And yet, even very recently, the Balearic Islands were havens of peace, untouched by any fundamental change; the Saracen norias are still turning today, and the peasants are still using the same type of plough as the Roman farmers.

Between the two extremes of modernity and archaism one thing remains constant – the setting, with all its light and fragrance.

If you come by boat from Marseilles or Barcelona – and it cannot be said too often, the most exciting way of reaching an island is by sea, however tiring the journey may be – the magic begins as you round the island of Dragonera. This generally happens at dawn, after a night crossing on one of the white steamships. You pass close to the *mola* of Andraitx and then comes more than an hour of watching and wondering, as you slowly progress along the shores which shimmer like jewels in the rising sun. Groves of olive and almond trees and forests of pines distil their fragrance in the dew, and the faint fleeting perfumes, mingled with the scent of the sea, even waft across the deck of the slowly wakening ship. It is a feast for all the senses. Your skin is caressed by a light breeze. The Mediterranean morning has begun. You seem to hear the cry of the *Jeune Parque* of Paul Valery :

> 'Greetings, O gods of rose-scent and salt-tang,
> First playthings of the newborn light
> O Islands ! . . .'

One last islet, Bull Island; one last cape, Calafiguera, and the bay of Palma flashes into sight. You feel the delicious shock which comes at the sight of a very few places like the Piraeus, Naples, or Istanbul. . . . With its engines shut off, the boat glides over the limpid water; the cathedral appears, lofty and delicate, and the horizons as they widen give promise of delights to come. The light has become stronger; in the distance the beaches stretch their white arms in welcome. Then the ship slackens speed and comes alongside, and the familiar hubbub of disembarkment begins. There was nothing in this arrival to inspire any self-conscious flights of lyricism: no Vesuvius, no Acropolis; only a port, a bay, a town with its outlines gradually growing clearer against the sky, only colours, scents and sounds. It is the beginning of a thrilling adventure: the discovery of a group of islands which, by its variety, can build up for us an amazing picture of what Mediterranean civilization means.

Chapter II

ITINERARIES

MAJORCA

THIS is the largest island and the one most frequently visited. It has an area of 1,405 square miles, that is almost two-thirds of the whole archipelago (which has an area of 1,936 square miles).

Following at random the roads radiating outwards from Palma, the traveller receives a set of very greatly differing impressions. If he goes westwards he passes the luxury hotels of the Paseo Maritimo at the foot of the hill of Bellver which give the capital all the appearance of a great modern city; then the road winds round *calas* and beaches, and leaves the sea, to cut across the headlands of Magaluf and Santa Ponsa, coming back to it among the pine forests of Paguera. There is a great temptation to wander idly along the bays which follow one upon the other as far as the bay of Puerto de Andraitx. The village, a few miles inland at the end of a wide valley, is dominated by the castle – now a museum – and the church. From Andraitx to Estellenchs the coast road has some very impressive views of tremendous cliffs and the sea.

The extensive work which has been undertaken to bring into prominence the wild beauty of what is known here as 'the Costa Brava' includes the opening to tourists of all these miles of winding roads and steep cliffs, which began less than five years ago. In this island with all its enchanting seductive beauty, the road from Andraitx to Estellenchs is probably one of the most fantastic to be found anywhere. After the pass of Sa Gremola the pine-bordered road leads to the belvedere at Ricardo Roca, then past Bañalbufar to the tower of Las Animas. A road winding through terraced farm-lands which are perhaps the most beautiful in the island, goes towards Valldemosa. Let yourself be tempted to follow it as far as the town of Soller; you will never tire of the sight of sea and rocks, and you will be all the more ready to appreciate the tranquillity of a beautiful land-locked bay.

Perhaps our traveller leaves Palma by the direct road to Soller. He follows a mountain stream towards its source, and his car stops at a level crossing. The gate-keeper's bell rings, and a little electric train flashes past, looking bright and new despite its age. About seven miles further on he stops to look at the gardens of Raixa; shortly afterwards he reaches the little village of Buñolas, dominated by limestone cliffs, and immediately after passing through it, comes upon the charming gardens of Alfabia. Then the road climbs up a real mountain pass with an interminable succession of hairpin bends. One more narrow gap, and the traveller emerges at that Pyrenean town of Soller, where it crouches, seeming out of all proportion, dwarfed by the vast amphitheatre of mountains surrounding it. The traveller presses on, and reaches Valldemosa by way of a coast road perched dizzily above the intensely blue sea. These are young mountains, born of geological cataclysms; there are waterfalls, deep scars in the vertical cliffs, terraced olive-groves. It is like the Corniche at Eze, or the Cote d'Azur – but fifty years ago, before the hotels were built. Near Son Marroig, the huge home of Archduke Salvador, is the belvedere which offers the best view of that strangely perforated point called La Foradada.

At Valldemosa the typical Mediterranean mountain scenery returns. The hills are spiky and barren; there are limestone peaks, orange and lemon groves, waterfalls giving birth to little mountain streams, gardens scenting the air, pine-woods like green splashes on the landscape, and the village itself, with its sloping streets, huddled around the church.

From Soller, the tourist should not hesitate to make for the monastery of Lluch, and even, on the way, to go as far down as the mouth of Torrente de Pareis, through the strange landscape of *calas* like gashes in the rocky surface. After visiting the monastery of Lluch where the *Morenata*, the Brown Virgin, is venerated, he should carry on to Pollensa.

At Pollensa, in the narrow village streets, when the landscape is no longer obscured by jagged lines of roofs, there is a feeling of gentleness, of harmony, which seems to belong to Tuscany. Perhaps the chief element of this comparison is to be found in the 365 steps leading to the *calvario*. The steps, which go up to a little oratory, are bordered by two parallel rows of cypresses. On Good Friday evening the procession of penitents each carrying a taper, stretches up the whole flight of steps and down again into the church.

About six miles away, Puerto Pollensa offers the idyllic landscape dear to Francis de Miomandre; it is also the starting point for excursions to Formentor, by boat, round the spur which hides the tip of the peninsula. Sometimes, with the effect of changing light, the landscape takes on strange dreamlike shapes; the mountain crests which dominate Puerto Pollensa and continue as far as the headland of Formentor look like Punch's hump, or like waves of stone, or like prehistoric monsters. And then, with a sudden contrast, the road slopes down again to that haven of peace and beauty, the beach and gardens of Formentor.

We reached Pollensa by the coast road. But the most direct route from Palma is the one passing through Santa Maria and the town of Inca, which is famous for its footwear industry, across a plain of which every plot is cultivated, with those kingly trees, the almond – sometimes as far as the eye can see – the fig-tree, and, in the more arid parts and on higher ground, the olive. And we must not forget one more Mediterranean tree, majestic in bearing – the carob-tree.

If we leave the main road for a few miles, we can plunge once more into the hills at the foot of the Sierra, and we will soon reach Selva, where an imposing flight of steps leads up to the church.

The road from Inca to Alcudia, to which we now return, runs across the plain, which during the Tertiary era was the sea-bed, and is covered with fertile red alluvial soil. Part of the plain is devoted to cereal crops and dotted with large farming villages: Puebla Muro, whose inhabitants swarm out into their fields in the morning and return at evening worn out, sitting on top of their farm-carts overflowing with corn, in the shadow of the bladed wheels of the wind-pumps, which stand side by side like enormous sunflowers swept by the wind. Part of it is covered with almond trees that rise from the red earth so close and intermingled that Queen Victoria on a visit once exclaimed: 'I believe it would be possible to go from one end of Majorca to the other by jumping from tree to tree.' This is the heart of the islands, the most productive part, with its large, austere, well-to-do villages. There are few tourists here; people work too hard.

Alcudia, the *Pollentia* of the ancients, has kept most of its walls. It was once a Roman colony, and its interesting features include two gates – that of San Vicente, by which the main road enters the town, and the more massive gate of El Muelle – the skilfully excavated remains of a Roman theatre, and, in the immediate neighbourhood, Puerto d'Alcudia, in the extreme north of the arc formed by the vast bay of the same name, which was the source of the town's prosperity. The road follows the shore in a very wide semicircle, reaches Ciudad Blanca, then runs for several miles between the sea and the lagoon.

Then we are at Ca'n Picafort with its burial grounds full of Roman tombs; leaving it behind, we drive through magnificent pine forests towards Arta, a mediaeval town which makes a striking impression when you catch sight of its castle on the summit of a hill overlooking the plain, with the town clustering round its feet as though round a pedestal.

Capdepera has the same effect. Do not hesitate to climb the steps leading to the castle ruins (it is also possible to get there by car, as a road winds up the side of the mountain); there is a most beautiful view to be seen from there. There is a deep feeling of peace, and the sea is in sight at nearby Cala Ratjada, a little port with a quaintness all its own in spite of the tourists.

It is impossible to talk about this part of the island without mentioning the caves. Earth movements and the eroding effects of running water have given rise to innumerable underground hollows; Majorca has as many holes as a Gruyere cheese. All along the coast, visitors can see the fantastic rugged shapes into which natural forces have carved the stone. Some of the caves were studied at the beginning of this century by the French geologist Martel. Much has been written about the delicacy of the stone columns and the strange plant and animal shapes which give the Majorcan caves the appearance of an underground Alhambra.

A few miles further south, at one of the extreme points of the peninsula, are the caves of Arta, a fairy palace made by nature, the beauty of which is enhanced by clever lighting. Near by, the eye is held by an ochre-yellow mass which gleams like the milk-white stalactites and stalagmites of the caves of Arta. This is the great square tower of Cañamel.

It is a landscape of low hills, and 'fjords' smoothed by the sea; the coast is of soft limestone deeply carved by thousands of years of erosion by the sea, in the same way as the Minorcan coast. Towards Porto Cristo there is sometimes a more welcoming type of inlet, the *cala* or cove, where the warm waves, clear as the waters of the Pacific, expend their last strength on the white sand, while on the ridge above them the wind whistles through a clump of pines; the *calas* where the smugglers once landed their goods, today the happiest of hunting grounds for those interested in undersea fishing.

It is never possible in Majorca to make a simple round tour if we do not want to miss out any of its marvels. On leaving the caves of Arta we might be tempted to go straight to Manacor, the second largest town in the island, where furniture and artificial pearls are made, and to return directly from there to Palma. But it would be a terrible mistake to miss out Porto Cristo, where the quay runs along a very beautiful *cala* with branches cut deep into the rocky plateau in different directions. And it would be no less a mistake to forget the caves of Hams, or the Caves of the Dragon which are even larger, and a part of which is visited by boat.

We can now return to Palma by way of Manacor, following the road which passes through Algaida, from whence we can get to the monastery of Randa. But we can do this only one one condition; we must, the next day, take another eastbound road, which goes to Lluchmayor, and visit the *calas* of the south-east coast: Porto Colom, Cala d'Or, Cala Santañy and Cala Figuera. On the way we absolutely must stop at Felanitx and see the magnificent flights of steps in front of the impressive façade of the church, and, close by, the hill crowned by the castle of Santueri. The summit is only 1,640 feet high, but rising as it does above the plain, it looks much more.

The tour we have just made is a very rapid one. It would be silly to rush it too much. It is better to take it slowly and intersperse it with days, or at least hours, of complete rest by the sea, in one or other of the *puertos* and *calas* which welcome us so kindly.

Back in Palma, we can go and have another look at some detail of the cathedral or some *patio* in the old town, which we have only glimpsed for a moment and of which we long to know more. If we have a little more time, we can not only stroll along the *Paseo Generalisimo*, but dawdle in the park of Bellver Castle and among the maze of narrow streets in the upper town.

MINORCA

Minorca is a paradox in itself, a sort of fragment of Brittany isolated in the Mediterranean. The ancient hills with their gentle rounded outlines filed smooth by countless aeons, are swept by the same winds as blow over the menhirs on the heathlands of Armorica. Here too there are megaliths, the *talayots* and *taulas*. As in Sardinia, the landscape is patterned by the drystone walls which form the estate boundaries, and by the beautiful farms with their herds of black and white cows, all small in size. They too remind one of Brittany.

By boat we arrive at Mahon, the capital, at the eastern tip of the island, and by air at the neighbouring aerodrome of San Luis.

Mahon is an astonishing place. Seen from the sea it is simply a cliff topped by a row of houses about half a mile long. As we approach we become aware of the fantastic shapes eroded in the rock; and suddenly we see the monumental flight of steps of l'Abundancia which leads up to the town from the port. Narrow streets, white houses, the church of Santa Maria, the church of the Carmen, the cloister of which has been turned into a market, a museum where archaelogical finds are shown, and a few wide streets one of which is called Orfila after the town's greatest man.

Nearby San Luis was founded by the French in the eighteenth century, and has become a holiday centre; Villa Carlos, to the south, has an immense square, from which the streets lead out with the regularity of the English military camp which it once was. Between Mahon and Villa Carlos, on the edge of the cliff, are great hotels built only a few years ago, with swimming pools of a brilliant blue. A little further off, but very near the road to the aerodrome, at Trepuco, is one of the most impressive megalithic monuments, consisting of a *taula* 14 feet high up to the horizontal slab, and a *talayot*, the whole standing inside a vast circle surrounded by a low drystone wall. Within there are fragments of other monuments.

We suggested coming by sea, and the first sight of Mahon is all that we have said. But the return journey should be made by air; it would be a pity to miss seeing from above the twelve-mile channel which has justly been compared with that of Brest.

Minorca is crossed from east to west by the road twenty-eight miles long which joins Mahon to the other capital of Ciudadela.

On the way we can see the white town of Alayor, lying close to the ground; its streets are quiet, and a few beautiful *patios* come as a surprise. Further on at Mercadal, the road divides off to go to Fornells and the cape which bounds the very deep inlet of the same name. We have found so many creeks to admire in the Balearic Islands, but this one seems particularly unforgettable. There is yet another which will impress us in the same way, as we shall find when we reach Ciudadela. We cross the town by means of a very curious street with a double row of arcades; looking down a side-street we see the chapel of the Rosary at one side and the facade of the cathedral at the bottom, and then we are in the great square of El Borne, bordered on one side by the Torresaura palace and on another by the Ayuntamiento. Then at last, leaning over the northern wall of the square, we suddenly see, far below, the branched inlet which became the port and thus gave birth to the town.

Evening is falling; the water sparkles in the setting sun. It is a strange sight, this narrow, enclosed inlet, brightly lit by the sun behind it. Where it meets the sea, a new hotel has just been completed – yet another! Its swimming pool is already shimmering in the light. In Minorca too, building goes on with feverish haste.

The *naveta of Es Tudons* is very close, by the side of the road by which we return to Mahon. It is a stone construction in the form of inverted boat, and is certainly worth seeing. Near Mahon the megaliths are the *taula* and the *talayot*; here it is the *naveta*; and here and there we can see a very large number of other fragments of monuments belonging to one or other of these types. This accumulation gives rise to the idea that the island must have been of some importance during the period when the megaliths were built.

The skill of the people in drystone building at all periods in its history is one of the main characteristics of Minorca. The fields are systematically bounded by low walls which give a distinctive character to the landscape.

IBIZA

Arriving at Ibiza by sea is very different from arriving at Mahon. Ibiza, on the island of the same name, is a bay, a pier delimiting the harbour, with light-houses at its end, and rocks. In front of us stands a citadel; this is the upper town, dominated by its fortifications and the cathedral. The lower town is spread out around the harbour, which is bordered along the whole of its length by a wide avenue. Close by is the *plaza mayor*, a square called Vara de Rey after a general who was born at Ibiza and fought in Cuba during the War of Independence. One of the streets leading out of it crosses the moat which formed part of the fortifications, passes beneath the Puerta de Las Tablas, which is adorned with Roman carvings, climbs up a steep slope and ends in the cathedral square near the museum which is extremely rich in Phoenician and Carthaginian relics. From this great height there is an unforgettable view over the fortifications, the roofs of the town, the port and the sea.

A peculiarity of the island is that all roads radiate outwards from Ibiza. Let us take the one going westwards: it leads to San Jorge and the salt-works, which have been one of the main sources of wealth throughout the island's history. We come back to the church of San Jorge and go on to San José. It is Easter Day, and we arrive in time for Mass. We see a crowd of men in black suits – looking like the inhabitants of any Continental town – and of middle-aged and elderly women wearing the much-photographed black dress and bodice and a voluminous shawl of embroidered silk or black damask, against which the brightly-coloured ribbon bow tying the plait stands out vividly. Not long ago these women wore their gold ornaments – the *empedades* – which made them look like Oriental or

Phoenician goddesses. And the girls? They walk to and fro, arms round each other's waists, in long swaying lines, laughing. They are tastefully dressed in modern style, their complexions are fresh, but their eyes are slightly made up, and they walk on stiletto heels. They have abandoned their traditional dress in a much shorter time than the Breton girls. Progress is swift in the Balearic Islands, and this justifies the existence of their very well-organized groups of folk-singers and dancers.

A good road goes from San José down to San Antonio, which stands on a very wide bay where even the most imposing houses – and some of them, especially the hotels, are very large indeed – do not seem to dwarf the impressive natural scenery. It is a charming city, and a city of the future with its wide avenues and great hotels.

We must return to Ibiza in order to go to San Miguel, a village perched on a hill, with a fortified church in which the villagers could take refuge in an emergency. We shall come back almost to Ibiza once more when we take the road leading to San Juan Baptista and the *cala* of Portinatx. It is a magnificent sight this bay – so very calm, with just a few houses and hotels to show that the tourist trade is beginning here too. We need not worry – space is limitless, and it will be a long time before man fills it completely.

We have to retrace our steps one last time and take the right fork for San Eulalia. The detour is well worth the trouble, for San Eulalia overlooks a golden beach, and its church, standing at the highest point of the town, is most interesting, having in front of it a cloister with a double row of arches placed in pairs, a sort of covered eyrie large enough for the crowd to remain outside the church even during an alarm.

Ibiza has been called the great discovery of recent years. The epithet is well-deserved, and the visitor who succumbs to its charm is happy indeed.

To look at, Ibiza is completely individual. The white cube-shaped houses clustered around the cathedral have an exotic appearance. Yes, indeed they remind us of North Africa, particularly Morocco. But they might also belong to those Greek towns we find on the Aegean. The light is more vivid than in Majorca. The countryside is dotted with whitewashed farms, austere in architecture, with windowless walls protecting against the heat. These white walls give the island the appearance of an oasis in the middle of the Mediterranean.

Crossing the narrow strait, we see that Formentera has some features very like those of its neighbour, but since there is not one single point in the island from which we cannot see or hear the sea, it is so very obviously an island that this has its effect on both the landscape and the way of life of the inhabitants.

The towns too have their landscapes – Palma, full of life and bustle; Ibiza, with its houses huddled together like any Moorish city; Inca and Manacor, swarming with a mass of humanity like the towns of Sicily.

We can walk down a narrow street in a port like Puerto Pollensa, away from the sea-front where the coaches take up too much room at certain times of day;

or we can look behind the great hotels or in the fishermen's quarters of Palma; and there we can push aside the mosquito netting and go into some *bodega* or *celler* to nibble *tapas* with our before-dinner drink; we have a choice of cuttlefish, stuffed mussels, tripe, kidneys, olives, served in little white oval dishes. We can sit at a white marble-topped table and drink muscatel or *palo*, the spirit distilled from carob-beans. With any luck a few musicians will soon come in; two guitarists and a singer, perhaps, who will at once strike up the best-known folk melodies, which mainly come from a deep-rooted peasant tradition, but in some cases have been picked up during a brief call in some Levantine port. Then to the rhythm of the *bolero mallorquin*, the whole tavern dances to a captivating exotic melody which resembles both the folk-tunes of Andalusia and the *bouzoukis* of Greece which we know from the famous *Children of the Piraeus*.

If we approach the Balearic Islands in this way we can have some inkling of the variety to be found there. A tour of these islands is as good as a tour of the whole Mediterranean. We are, however, on Spanish soil; and everywhere, except perhaps in Majorca where the English occupation has left a tinge of Protestantism among the inhabitants, the Catholic church takes up a large part of the life of towns and villages. To the traveller entering the harbour of Palma, the cathedral appears to dominate the town. The sun gilds its stones from dawn to dusk, and its lines flow in perfect harmony. 'It is not the spiky forest-like structure, full of nooks and crannies, that we find at Rheims or Chartres . . . at one glance, the eye takes in the whole of this vast building.'[1]

In even the most humble of villages the church tower broods over the delicate symmetry of tiled roofs huddled in its shade. And then there is a less lofty architecture – that of cloisters, like those of San Francisco in Palma. There, a rectangular arcade surrounds a garden of palms and roses; in the centre of the rectangle is a well with a carved lip surmounted by a design in wrought iron work. There are a few benches where travellers can sit and luxuriate in a silence which must be one of the greatest delights of the world. A flight of doves stirs the warm air with its wings. From time to time the air thrills with the sound of the organ coming from the church where lie the earthly remains of the blessed Doctor Illuminatus. Perhaps it is here, in all its intensity of feeling, that we draw nearest to the true soul of the Balearic Islands.

[1] Lavedan, *Palma de Majorque et les Iles Baléares*, Paris 1936.

Chapter III

THE STORY OF THE ISLANDS

THE DAYS OF ANTIQUITY

IT is history that will give us a clue to the deeply Mediterranean character of the islands. We do not need to be trained archaeologists; anyone who has visited the Isla Plana or the Puig des Molins on Ibiza, the megaliths of Es Tudons on Minorca, the tombs of Ca'n Picafort, the excavations near the church of Alcudia, or the Roman theatre and bridge at Pollentia on Majorca, has already had direct experience of places apt to call up at a glance the ancient past of the islands.

It is generally considered that up to the conquest of Metellus in 123 B.C. life in the Balearic Islands was governed by an old, simple form of civilization, not unlike that of Sardinia, which was not shaken by the invasions of either the Phoenicians or the Carthaginians. This point of view needs examining in more detail.

During the Bronze Age, corresponding in Spain to the period 1900-900 B.C., the stabilization of the native population, which came from Africa and probably occupied the islands at a relatively late date, appears to have taken place.[1] The culture known as El Argar developed in and around the mining province of Almeria, in the south-east of the Iberian peninsula, and seems to have spread to the Balearic Islands between 1600 and 1400 B.C. Various metal utensils related to those discovered on the Peninsula have been found on Majorca (around Felanitx, Cova dels Bous, Santa Maria and Lluchmayor, and Cas Hereu). Then a certain change affected the whole archipelago; this was the rise of the civilization of the *talayots* or megalithic constructions, which developed about 1100 B.C. and lasted almost five centuries. These buildings belong to a relatively prosperous era; they are the expressions of a fairly considerable population expansion. A thousand *talayots*, representing nearly two hundred villages, have been found in Majorca, and five hundred *talayots* in Minorca.[2] These remains have often been linked with the nuraghi of Sardinia; in fact the hypothesis of a Sardinian invasion of the Balearic Islands has even been considered. There were at that time a large number of exchanges by sea, including probable contacts with the sea-going powers of the eastern Mediterranean: the Lydians and perhaps even the Etruscans. The islanders were also in touch, by way of the

[1] After Bosch Gimpera, *La Formacion de los pueblos de España*, Mexico 1945.
[2] After Garcia Pericot, *L'Espagne avant la conquête romaine*, Paris 1952.

Atlantic sea-routes, with certain Northern peoples. The objects found on the site of 'Talaia Joana' near Las Salinas in Majorca consist, according to Bosch Gimpera, of flat bronze axes and necklaces of a Nordic type (*halskragen*). Relations with the Phoenicians and king Geryon began at the end of the ninth century and continued into the eighth. 'Geryon, idealized by the Greek legend of Heracles, appears to have ruled at that time over a kingdom[1] which included the Balearic Islands and seems to have carried on the ancient trade relations of Andalusia with the islands of the western Mediterranean including Sardinia.'[2] When the centre of gravity of the Phoenician empire moved from the Levant to Carthage the bond between it and the Balearic Islands became closer. The colony of Ebusus (Ibiza) was founded in 654. It was probably established in the first place for military purposes, as a base was needed on the route from Andalusia to Sardinia. This Carthaginian period did not prevent the island from being affected by other influences. In the sixth century the Phocaeans used the islands as ports of call.[3] Local craftsmen still produce various objects some of which, such as bronze bulls' heads, show that the influence of Crete still persists. The tombs of Son Real near Ca'n Picafort in Majorca date from a little later. The excavations, which have been going on since 1957, are revealing one of the most promising sites in the islands; they bear witness to the influence of sea-going peoples who came from the eastern Mediterranean between the fifth and third centuries B.C. They left a town of which only the burial-ground has so far been excavated; research has been possible on seventy-two tombs.

Elsewhere too, the large number of objects discovered suggests that the islands were relatively prosperous. There were families rich enough to have tombs built for themselves; the sites of the *talayots* were re-occupied, and about the fourth century B.C. there was probably a period of population growth. In the fourth and third centuries the Carthaginian armies used Balearic mercenaries. These 'Balearic slingers' whose reputation was equal to that of the Cretan archers, formed a picked body of men probably trained according to very ancient local methods. When Metellus landed in 123, he feared these hurlers of stones. The agnomen 'Balearicus' given to the Roman conqueror could have been due either to this conquest or to a campaign of pacification carried on against the pirates who infested these waters after the decline of Carthage. Strabo (Book III, 5) gives a fairly long description of the state of the islands on the arrival of the Romans, but we must admit that apart from three allusions to their fertility, the slingers and certain types of tunic, the text is extremely vague. The only definite information of interest which it gives concerns the founding of two colonies at Palma and

[1] Its capital was near Cadiz.
[2] Bosch Gimpera, *op. cit.*
[3] Carpenter in *The Greeks in Spain*, London 1925, links their coming with names ending in the suffix 'ussa': Melussa, in Minorca; Cromeussa, in Majorca; Pitiussa, in Ibiza; Ofiussa, in Formentera. He dates certain ancient bronzes, such as the *Athena Promarchos* of Majorca and two bronzes found in Minorca, from this 'Phocaean period'.

Pollentia, and especially that 'three thousand Romans from Iberia settled there'. During the war which Pompey carried on against the pirates in 67 B.C., L. Mancius Torquatus patrolled the coasts of the archipelago; at that time the Romans considered it both as a stopping place on the journey towards Spain and as a source of supply of the slingers who served as auxiliary troops in the wars under Caesar in Gaul, and under Sulla in Africa against Jugurtha; these are the troops immortalized in a bas-relief on Trajan's Column. During these centuries of *pax Romana* the texts scarcely mention the islands; their last appearance dates from the fourth century A.D. Under Theodosius (about 380) they were elevated to the status of a Roman province.

These two thousand years appear to have seen a succession of civilizations superimposed on the most ancient culture, that of the *talayots*: a Carthaginian element, a definite Hellenic influence, and lasting traces of Roman occupation. But each time, the islands form part of a political or economic whole of which they are not the centre. Only in the Middle Ages did they reach this never-to-be-repeated stage in their history.

THE KINGS OF MAJORCA

The Conquest of the Islands

The Christian faith was introduced at a relatively late date. Majorca acquired a bishopric in the course of the fifth century. Minorca and Ibiza also obtained the right to their own episcopal seat at approximately the same time; this stresses the fact that even for such short distances between islands, travel by sea was fraught with real risks. The Christian religion of this period was characterized by an early form of monasticism. Traces have been found in Cabrera of a community of Augustinian monks under the pontificate of Saint Gregory the Great.[1] But the presence of these anchorites is no indication that the Balearic Islands were densely populated or prosperous in the seventh century; the Vandals, who, under their king Gonderic, conquered the islands in 421, had completely ravaged them, wiping out almost every trace of Roman civilization. The Goths followed, and Belisarius was able to wrest the islands from their grasp in about 550 and re-attach them to the Empire for only a very short time. This appears to explain the relative scarcity of Roman ruins. Then came the first typical Moslem invasion, in 713.

For five centuries the islands were occupied by the Saracens, apart from a few short breaks. They thus had time to leave a lasting impression; they fashioned the land in their own image, leaving for the tourist of today something more than tangible souvenirs: an atmosphere, traditions, even place-names (Binisalem, Biniali, Alcudia). They left also monuments and the innumerable *norias* which are still turning today; their methods of building and of tilling the soil still remain. But for a long time the only activity they carried on was piracy. From

[1] cf. Dameto, *op. cit.*

their first conquest onwards they used the Balearic Islands as an operational base for their raids on the Levantine side of the Continent. Eginhard[1] tells us that Charlemagne sent his son Pepin to attack the Moors and that this 'pacification' was successful. However, about the middle of the ninth century the Genoese, like the good merchants they were, handed the islands over to the Mohammedan kings of Bona in return for substantial advantages in kind. The islands, placed thus at the mercy of the pirates from the south, then suffered from the invasion of men from the north, the Normans. The period that followed was a dark one for the five islands.

It was not until the eleventh century that the Balearic Islands became firmly attached to the Moslem world. At this period they formed part of a maritime kingdom including Marinia (the coast between Denia and Alicante). The port of Denia was at that time a regular centre of scientific learning. Politically, the little state owed its glory to the work of Emir Mochelid who sailed from the Balearic Islands to conquer Sardinia.

It was then that an important change took place in the Christian world – the spread of the crusading spirit. Wonderful perspectives of conquest over Islam appeared on every hand. A Catalan prince, the Count of Urgel, seems to have tried to fight against the Moors. Raymond Berenger III, Count of Barcelona, was the first to make an effective attempt; he took Ibiza and Majorca with the help of Genoa, Pisa, Montpellier and Narbonne. But when the Saracens attacked Barcelona, Raymond Berenger had more urgent matters to attend to; he left the defence of the island to the seamen of Genoa, who 'came to an arrangement' with the Moslems there and then, and sold them all that Raymond Berenger had so hardly won (1115-1116). From then onwards there was a continual struggle between the Moorish rulers of Palma and the Christian rulers of Barcelona. The invasion of the Almohades did not basically change the relationships between the islands and the mainland. However the Moslem side was weakened by internal struggles (to such an extent that on several occasions the ruler of Palma called on the Aragonese for help), and there were occasionally some very odd expeditions going on. For example, from this period dates an adventure with which the Majorcans are rarely credited: the conquest of Ifrikya.

In 1184 a regular Armada put to sea, consisting of two hundred horsemen and four thousand infantry embarked in thirty-two ships. The Almoravide fleet successfully attempted a landing on the coasts of their mortal enemy, the Almohade Empire. At the head of the expedition were two Moslem 'conquistadores', Ali and Yahia ben Ghanya, who undertook to attack the Almohades on their own ground. The start of this expedition, which was perhaps bolder from a technical point of view than the landing of the Christians on Majorca which took place the following century, has been studied in detail.[2] These are the broad outlines of the campaign:

[1] Eginhard, *Oeuvres complètes*, Paris 1840-1843 (pp. 238-242).
[2] Alfred Bel, *Les Benou Ghânyà*, Paris 1903.

The squadron reached Bougie on November 13, 1184, and the town fell immediately. It was the fleet—mainly consisting of Majorcan ships—which made it possible to establish firm communications between the base and the bridge-head gained on the Maghrib. For the next twenty years the war spread all along the coast, even going beyond the bounds of Tunisia: Gabes, Tripoli and even Constantine fell into the hands of the Majorcan conquerors; Tunis itself fell in 1205. Territories gained were held until the death of Yahia el Mayorqui, as the Africans called him, in 1238. One of the most surprising aspects of this adventure is that it was carried on while the Balearic Islands were actually changing hands; Majorca was taken by the Almohades in 1203, then by the Christians in 1229. This brings out in a curious way the fact that before the Christians came the Balearic Islands were involved in maritime expeditions to distant parts; there must, then, have been a formidable Majorcan navy as early as the end of the twelfth century.

The islands were retaken by the Almohades in 1203, as witness a large number of trade agreements with the Pisans and the Genoese. The translations of Arab chronicles are no less interesting to read than the stories of the Christian conquest. They tell of the same kind of life, the same reverses, the same epic battles. The only difference is in the bearing of events. Even reduced to more modest proportions, the affair of 1229—the conquest of James I—marks an important stage in the reconquest of the islands by the Christians and in the development of the crusading spirit.

What was the situation in the island of Majorca before the reconquest?

The Arabs of Majorca were mostly farmers; there were a large number of small farms, and the cultivated area extended right up to the mountains. According to Lecoy de La Marche[1] more than eighty water mills were working around Palma; the Moors, making wonderful use of the fertility of the land, were exporting wheat and flour. Through treaties concluded with the Pisans and the Genoese, this trade was extended to the whole of the western Mediterranean. The Balearic Islands served as a kind of turntable between the merchant cities of the Christian parts of the coast and the ports of the Maghrib. In the middle of the twelfth century the geographer El Idrisi said this of the Balearic Islands: 'The island of Ibiza is pretty, planted with vines and very productive of grapes; we see a town there, small, but pleasant and well populated. . . . At the east of this island, and a day's journey away is the island of Majorca; its capital city is large, and the prince who governs it commands a large garrison and has plenty of arms and resources at his disposal. Also to the east we may see the island of Minorca, situated opposite Barcelona, a day's journey away; the voyage from Minorca to the island of Sardinia takes four sailing days.'[2]

Little remains today of this prosperity in the way of tangible relics. The palace of the Emirs of Palma was the Almudaina; the quarter of the town surrounding

[1] *Les Relations publiques de la France et du royaume de Majorque*, 2 vols., Paris 1892.
[2] A. Bel, *op. cit.*

36

it was enclosed by a wall. Near the cathedral an arch spanning a narrow street (Calle de la Almudaina) can still be seen today. Also at Palma, near the church of Santa Clara, there are a few surviving fragments of baths which tradition attributes to the Moslem period. However, a more objective study suggests that these ruins are just as likely to date from the Jewish as from the Islamic period,[1] but as far as materials are concerned, it is thought that these buildings were made from old stone blocks dating from the Visigothic period. There, as archaeological finds stand at the moment, the list of 'Arab' remains stops short. As for the actual functioning of this civilization grafted upon the Balearic Islands, there is no doubt that it was characterized by a luxurious and often sensual way of life (several Christians possessed harems); the frequent difficulties about Christian prisoners, together with the rape of women and continual acts of piracy must inevitably have annoyed the inhabitants of the mainland. Add to all this a certain psychological climate on the mainland; hate against Islam was being whipped up by the exploitation of legends such as those of Charlemagne and the Cid, and then came the victory of Las Navas de Tolosa (1212). The conquest of Majorca was a great step towards the crumbling of the whole Moorish domination over the Iberian peninsula; it is far more than a mere feat of arms without historical consequences.

The incident occurred in 1228; in the course of the raids and counter-raids carried on by the two powers, two ships of James of Aragon carrying archers were taken. The king of Aragon sent a ship with an envoy on board[2] to negotiate for the liberty of the imprisoned crews. The Genoese, Pisan and Provençal merchants advised the Emir Mohammed of Palma to stand firm, mainly for reasons of self-interest, as they feared their Catalan competitors might gain too much advantage in what they considered their own preserve. The Emir sent word to James that he would give up nothing, 'neither men nor gods, and that he cared nothing for his challenge'.

The situation was an explosive one, but it remained for the Christian ruler to organize a military operation against the man who had insulted him. Matters were precipitated by the combination of religious motives and certain commercial interests; the merchants in particular whipped up the enthusiasm of the knights: 'One of those who carried most weight in the city, Peter Martell, went so far as to invite James I, at Tarragona, to a sumptuous banquet where the affair was to be officially considered'.[3] In the course of this orgy, Martell described to the king the enchanting beauty of Majorca. The guests, 'fascinated by the words of this old sailor who was showing them a real Promised Land, begged the king to snatch so fair a domain from the grasp of the infidels and to lead them to the conquest of the Balearic Islands; the Christian faith, they said, would be exalted, and the whole universe would admire this twenty-year-old prince in quest of a

[1] cf. P. Lavedan, *op. cit.*
[2] James Sanz of Montpellier.
[3] Lecoy de la Marche, *op cit.*

kingdom in the middle of the sea'. James replied: 'Your proposition pleases me above all things; it rests only with me not to let it fail, and may God help us.'[1]

Immediately afterwards the Cortes met in Barcelona (December 1228). The ecclesiastics, nobles, and even some bourgeois, who were qualified to sit, voted considerable means to the king. On December 23, 1228, the decisions were formally recorded, and a contract was signed between the king and the leading figures of the kingdom. James was to set off on the campaign in May and distribute to his subjects the lands, castles, domains and estates taken from the infidels. They were certainly counting their chickens before they were hatched, but the fact that a scheme for the distribution of the booty had been drawn up was a great help to the king in recruiting knights, unemployed sailors, and adventurers in search of fortune. So as not to spoil the chances of complete success, the preparations took a very long time; they were ready about the middle of August. Even the Templars promised to help in the affair in return for 'the gift for the king of the palace of the Jews called the Almudaina, with a piece of land and a port situated outside the town'.[2]

To the 680 knights and their 10,000 servants, foot-soldiers and squires who made up the bulk of the expedition, we have to add a large number of other participants, in particular 'foreigners', that is to say nobles from Aragon and from the South of France – from Roussillon like Bernard de Montesquiou, from Foix like N. Bovraz, from Navarre like N. d'Aigremont, from Languedoc (a very large contingent) like several of the Barbaïra clan of the seneschalsy of Carcassonne, Bernard Liret of Narbonne etc.; lords of Montpellier like Berenguer Cayzan, captain of the royal ship; citizens of Marseilles like Gombert Baldovi and Raymond Poquet; Provençaux like Jean le Sol (an armourer who equipped two ships at his own expense), Hugues de Forcalquier, etc. Of course this brief list is only of interest if we consider that these knights founded families in the Balearic Islands and thus achieved something more than a temporary hold over them. They wove bonds between the south of France and these islands far stronger than those arising from any similarity of landscape or way of life.

The king's army had a total strength of roughly 20,000 men divided into four corps, with in addition 1,500 horses. The fleet consisted of twenty-five large vessels, eighteen tartanes (transport vessels for horses and machines), twelve fighting ships and about a hundred other boats of various types.

This expedition which we should today consider international because of the frontiers dividing our maps, sailed from Salou in the province of Tarragona, at dawn on Wednesday, September 15, 1229. It was a veritable Armada of the Mediterranean, setting out on an amazing adventure. At the start of the crossing, before the ordeal, the king, rather like some Shakespearean hero going into battle, began his journal of the campaign. We can imagine him on board his

[1] *ibid.*   [2] *ibid.*

ship, sailing before the wind through the warm starry night, the sea murmurous about him, writing these notes by the light of a lantern that swayed with the vessel's movements: 'We are going on this voyage to defend the faith and fight the unbelievers. Our purpose is twofold: to convert these pagans and to bring back their kingdom to the true allegiance of God. And since we march in His name, we are confident; He will lead us.'[1]

The geography of the island was such that the Moslems would not easily be taken by surprise. Today, when we follow the beautiful Costa Brava from Dragonera to Soller, we can easily imagine that sentries would be very quickly aware that a fleet of that size was approaching. What is more, we should not forget that the mustering of 20,000 men over the space of six months is not an operation which can be completed without something leaking out.

The fleet had already survived a storm, and the landing was to take place in the region of the Bay of Pollensa, but for various reasons (a large number of reefs?) it was decided to make land elsewhere. The squadron sailed right along the part of the coastline facing Catalonia and touched land in the creek known today by the name of San Telmo, near S'Arraco. On Friday, September 7th, after a crossing lasting thirty-six hours, the king's ships, says the chronicle, made a landfall on the islet of Pantalleu. The whole fleet arrived on Saturday the 8th and Sunday the 9th, the first reconnaissances took place along the coast; 15,000 Moors and Majorcans were assembled there, but there was treachery. A major-domo of the Emir of Palma, named Ali, prostrated himself before the king and gave him some important information on the Moors' defence plans. James changed his tactics and landed an attacking party commanded by Raymond Murcade at Santa Ponsa (near what is now the seaside resort of Paguera) cutting off the Moorish vanguard from the road to Palma. The landing was successful, and the first engagement accounted for 1,000 Moors dead or wounded. On Tuesday the 11th all remaining troops landed at Parosa, nearer to Palma. The Emir had lost the first skirmishes, and his forces were scattered along the coast, but he still had a large force at the entrance of the Bay of Palma. The decisive battle took place on the 12th of September, and the account of it given in James's chronicles is as terrible as any ancient epic.

It was a fierce battle, long undecided. The king lost some of his best knights. Much blood was shed, but the result was of capital importance; the exterior defences of Palma were breached. On the evening of the 13th, James was encamped at 'Bendinat'.[2] On the 14th the fleet sailed into the harbour and blocked the way out. The army in its turn was surrounding the walls, and instead of pitched battles there was a stage of siege for three and a half months. Considering the means at their disposal at that time it is no exaggeration to say

[1] Chronicles of James I, chapter LIV.
[2] We remember the extremely debatable play on words which is commonly advanced as the origin of this name: 'I have dined well' in Majorcan dialect. But perhaps we should look further for its origin, in the Arabic prefix *ben*.

that it was carried on with great skill. From a military point of view the besieged were superior; the balance of power was tipped by a 'psychological' factor. The Arab governor of the Pollensa district, Ben Abet, surrendered to James; he was one of the most powerful military leaders, and his submission gave the king of Aragon the mastery of the whole of the northern part of the island. The Emir adopted the most cruel methods of defence, but could not prevent the inevitable; on December 31st the final attack was made, and the last pocket of resistance, the Almudaina, was taken; the Christian prisoners were freed. According to the Catalan chroniclers there were 20,000 dead; according to Arab witnesses at least 80,000 victims. D'Esclot speaks of 50,000.[1]

Thus the kingdom of the Balearic Islands entered into the bosom of the Christian church on Monday, December 31, 1229.

The conquest was followed by the occupation, during which the newly-won territory was absorbed into a different religious and political system. First of all the island was 'cleaned up'; there were battles to stamp out the last traces of Moorish military power at Inca and in the caves of Arta; and the other islands, on which many of the enemy had taken refuge, had still to be conquered. In 1231, Minorca came under the vassalage of James I as a result of negotiations carried on in very odd circumstances: the ambassador of the Christian ruler was negotiating at Ciudadela, while beacons were lit on the other side of the strait, a piece of bluff designed to give the illusion of a strong concentration of troops ready to attack Minorca. The island recognized James's political sovereignty, but clung to the Mohammedan faith; thus the Moors accepted a sort of mixed régime which was to protect them from the rigours of armed conquest (this lasted until 1287, the year in which Alfonso III of Aragon took possession of the island by force). As for Ibiza, it was simply annexed to the kingdom of Majorca in 1257 despite several attempts by the Moors to fight back. The re-population of Majorca began immediately after the conquest. All the members of the expedition were allowed to take up residence and received grants of land. Thus even 'foreigners' from Languedoc, Montpellier or Marseilles, were able to settle there.

By the will of James I, drawn up on August 21, 1262, the Balearic Islands took their place in world history as their future diverged from that of the Spanish provinces on the mainland. 'To his elder son, James bequeaths the kingdom of Aragon, to his younger son (Prince James) the kingdom of Majorca with Minorca and Ibiza, the counties of Roussillon, Cerdagne and their dependencies, the fiefs held in his name by the counts of Foix and Ampurias, the town of Collioure, Montpellier and its seigniory, and the viscounty of Carlat in Basse-Auvergne.'[2]

James, king and conqueror, died at Valencia on July 27, 1276, aged sixty-

[1] Bernard Desclot, quoted by Lecoy de la Marche.
[2] These possessions had been recognized by Saint Louis as belonging to Aragon in the Treaty of Corbeil, 1258.

eight. 'With his death, the independent kingdom of Majorca came definitely into being.'[1] Geographically, the state of Majorca falls into two parts. One part consists of the islands, and the other covers vast territories on the mainland.

James II

The period upon which the kingdom now entered began with serious trouble from the political point of view. On January 20, 1279, the elder and younger sons of James I, after what had very nearly become an armed conflict, signed a treaty by which the power of the kings of Majorca was considerably lessened in favour of the rulers of Aragon. This treaty, instead of allaying any fears, sowed the seeds of discord between the houses of Aragon and Majorca; 'it amounted to the setting aside of James I's will'. The rivalry of the two brothers went beyond the bounds of a mere family quarrel, and led to a struggle of much greater proportions; it was at this moment that the question of Sicily arose. Peter of Aragon, after the famous massacre of the Sicilian Vespers, was from a military point of view in quite a strong position. But he immediately came up against the opposition of the Holy See and of his ally the king of France. James II could not remain neutral: he appears to have sought an alliance with France in order to counterbalance the unfortunate effects of the treaty of Perpignan, signed on January 20, 1279. He very nearly had an extremely important part to play. He had the choice of joining the 'league' of princes allied with the Holy See, whose interests had been endangered in Sicily by the king of Aragon, or of taking the side of his brother, and he could have taken advantage of this fact to gain great territorial advantages and make the islands the key point, practically, of the whole Mediterranean. But his political sense was not keen enough. However, neutrality was impossible, and the affair of Montpellier (1281) finally decided which side he had to take; in order to prevent the town from falling into the hands of the Aragonese, he was obliged to ally himself with Philip the Bold. The affair itself was a result of the complex system of jurisdictions under which the town came. At this time the authority of the municipality and its officers, and that of the king of Majorca, the bishop and the king of France, all overlapped. The king of Majorca's lieutenant, Peter of Claramont, escaped narrowly when a mysterious attempt was made on his life, and a series of struggles began which went far beyond the confines of the town. It appears in fact that these troubles were caused by nothing more or less than the rival influences of Aragon, France and Majorca. Politically, the result was that the king of France received the homage of the king of Majorca and the two houses then allied themselves against Peter of Aragon, by the secret treaty of Carcassonne, August 16, 1283. By this treaty, the political future of the kingdom of the Balearic Islands was linked with that of Paris.

From the very beginning of military operations this provisional alliance fell short of expectations. Several reverses such as the siege of Gerona and the naval

[1] Lecoy de la Marche, *op. cit.*

Garonne

Toulouse

Lodève
Montpellier
Aigues-Mortes
Héranlt
Orb
Rhône
Pézenas
Béziers
Carcassonne
Aude

CAPCIR
CONFLENT
Perpignan
ROUSSILLON
Elne
CERDAGNE
Villefranche
Collioure
Port-Vendres
Puigcerdà
VALLESPIR

la Seu d'Urgell

C A T A L O N I A
AMPOURDA
Ampurias
Ter
Gerona
Rio Segre

Barcelona

M E D I T E R R A N E A N
S E A

B A L E A R I C   I S L A N D S

C. Formentor
Ciudadela
MINORCA
Castell del Rey
Mahon
Soller
Alcudia
Bellver
Sineu
Arta
I. Dragonera
Manacor
Andraitx
Palma
Campos
Felanitx
MAJORCA
Santañy
I. Cabrera

San Antonio
IBIZA
Ibiza
I. FORMENTERA

0   Kms.   100

2. *The Kingdom of Majorca.*

disaster in the Bay of Rosas, and above all the death of the French king at Perpignan on September 5, 1285, left the Majorcans alone against the Aragonese. In addition, thirty-six days after Philip the Bold, Peter of Aragon died, leaving his son Alfonso on the throne. James II's situation then became critical, for the Aragonese laid waste Majorca and Ibiza and even landed on Minorca in 1287, putting the Moors to flight. The damage done by Aragon was aggravated by the new policy of the new king of France, Philip the Fair: scarcely had he taken his place on the throne when he annexed Montpellier to his crown. After this show of force, Philip the Fair, having made use of the quarrel between James II and the Aragonese, decided to end it. They finally reached a 'triangular' settlement (Treaty of Anagni, 1295).

The most lasting historical consequence was the return of James II of Majorca to his own territory. During the last years of his reign (until 1311) the islands enjoyed a period of unequalled peace and prosperity. Agriculture was reorganized, and industry made considerable progress. He built castles to protect the coasts of his islands from pirate raids. During these sixteen years of political stability, an immense amount of work was accomplished. From an architectural point of view the fragments which have come down to us are very important; it was at this time that work on the cathedral was begun, the castle of Bellver and the church and cloister of San Francisco were built, and a new royal palace rose from the ruins of the palace of the Emirs. From this period, too, dates the protection given by the court of Majorca 'to the leading wing of the Church, the powerful orders of Franciscans and Dominicans'.[1] In the field of culture, this was the time of Majorca's great brilliance, with its college of Miramar and above all with the personality of Ramon Llull. And finally, the Balearic Islands achieved an economic expansion which we will give here in broad outline.

Palma was at that time a great port, permanently in touch with Valencia and Barcelona. Trade relations were established with the Moslem powers of northern Africa and even Syria and as far afield as Tartary. They did not limit their activities to the Mediterranean area; we can, it seems, consider them as among the first Mediterraneans to follow the Atlantic sea-routes and even enter the North Sea. They were enterprising enough to reach London as early as 1281. 'In the summer of 1281, three vessels from the Mediterranean put in carrying a cargo of English wool; one was the ship of Francesco (of Liguria), another that of Antonio de Mari, and the third was the galley of Guillen de Bone from "Mayhorke"; they were carrying 267 sacks of five stones of wool intended for Catalans and Provençaux.'[2]

Thus at the same time as the Genoese and long before the Venetians, the Majorcans played a leading part in the expansion of sea-routes and trade between the Mediterranean, and Asia and northern Europe at the end of the thirteenth century.

[1] M. Durliat, L'Art dans le royaume de Majorque, Toulouse 1962.
[2] C. Lopez, Revue belge de philologie, 1951, p. 1173.

The experience of the old sea-dogs with their more or less accurate memories, and the tales told by ambassadors to distant Asia, were augmented by the special knowledge of the Jewish scholars and merchants who were settling in Majorca throughout the thirteenth century. Specialists in economic history have clearly shown the stages in the economic expansion of the Aragonese and Majorcans, but what lasting result would these contacts with the subjects of the Shah of Persia or with the merchants of London have brought about if there had not been a particular psychological climate at that precise moment?

Traces of a large Jewish colony in the Balearic Islands do not appear much before the conquest of 1229; they apparently emigrated to Majorca from northern Africa in the middle of the thirteenth century as a result of persecutions suffered at the hands of the Almohades. It is not easy to tell their approximate numbers. An edict of James I issued on June 11, 1247, seems to indicate that they were fairly numerous. In this document the king accords protection to certain Jews from Morocco – especially Salomon ben Amar, a Jew from Sidgilmassa – and to all Jews, whatever their place of origin, who wish to settle in his domains of Majorca, Barcelona and Valencia, and forbids his subjects to molest them or do them harm in any way at all on penalty of very heavy fines. This measure, which appears so liberal, had really only one purpose; to attract intelligent and experienced merchants to the new confederation. As a result Jews came from all parts of the Mediterranean, some of them real scholars, such as 'Leo Mosconi, from Ochrida in Macedonia, fortunate possessor of a remarkable library some books of which were acquired at his death in Palma by the cartographers Cresques, father and son. Others were indefatigable travellers like Joseph Faquin, a Jew from Barcelona who, after travelling all over the world, came to settle in Majorca and take a wife.'[1] Thus in the last years of the reign of James II, Majorca was the centre of a cosmopolitan culture with its roots in the Levant, Macedonia and the Maghrib. We shall see how all these different elements took concrete form fifty years later.[2]

King Sancho, The Regency, The End of the Kingdom of Majorca

When James II died, the crown of Majorca fell to his second son Sancho, as James, the elder, had renounced all his rights to the throne and become a Franciscan monk. His thirteen-year reign was in striking contrast with that of his father; an almost complete freedom from political upheavals made it possible for the king to administer his affairs in perfect tranquillity. As his health was not

[1] G. de Reparaz, 'Activité commerciale du royaume d'Aragon au XIII⁰ siècle et son influence sur le développement de l'école cartographique de Majorque' (*Bulletin hispanique* vol. 49, no. 3-4, 1947).

[2] On the material position of the Jews in Majorca see *Notes et Documents pour servir à l'histoire des juifs des Baléares* by Morel Fatio, Paris 1882.

good, he chose to establish his principal residence at Valldemosa, where he built a palace of which nothing remains today; we know only that on its site was built the monastery where George Sand and Chopin stayed. Following his father's policy, which in the last years of the latter's reign consisted in steering a middle course between the interest of Aragon and France, he continued to build up the Majorcan fleet to a remarkable degree. Sometimes the ties of vassalage binding him to Aragon drew him into such expeditions as the conquest of Sardinia by the new king of Aragon James II. Since his marriage with Maria of Naples had not resulted in a male heir, the question of succession led to a serious political situation between him and the kingdom of Aragon. James II, in fact, claimed that by a clause in the will of James the Conqueror the kingdom was to revert to Aragon if Sancho had no sons. Sancho rejected this claim and took as his heir his nephew James III, the son of his brother Ferdinand. War very nearly broke out again between Sancho and James of Aragon, but the support of the king of France helped to avert any serious crisis. In 1324 the King of Majorca died at Perpignan, leaving a child of nine on the throne.

There was no question of a child as young as this reigning at Palma, especially in view of the traditional claims of Aragon. For this reason measures had been taken in Sancho's lifetime for the creation of a regency council made up of three citizens of Majorca, two of Perpignan and one of Puigcerda, to hold sway during the minority of the new king James III. Very soon the council found it was sharing its authority with an uncle of the young king: Philip, abbot of Saint-Martin-de-Tours. Although he had little experience of political intrigue, he had a brilliant success in 1325: James of Aragon had never given up his ambitions to annex Majorca; but Philip obtained from him a renunciation duly signed and sealed, and persuaded him to consent to a betrothal between the boy king of Majorca and a little girl of five, Constance, granddaughter of the king of Aragon. (However, this marriage did not provide a lasting solution, because, as we shall see, it was Constance's own brother who, after he became king of Aragon, drove her husband from the Majorcan throne.)

As a result of the betrothal of James III and Constance, the king of Majorca was in 1327 the son-in-law of the new king of Aragon, Alfonso IV (1327-1336), successor to James II. For about ten years the two formely rival houses lived on good terms with each other. The king of Majorca governed his kingdom effectively laying down precise rules for administration, government, etiquette and protocol.[1] In 1336 Alfonso died, leaving the crown of Aragon to his son Peter IV (known as Peter the Ceremonious) who was aged sixteen. The king of Majorca and the king of Aragon were brothers-in-law, but the difference in their characters was to result in the defeat and final eviction from the Majorcan throne of the elder, James III.

The political ambitions of Peter IV were mainly centred on Castille and the Balearic Islands. Leaving out of account the difference in character, the king of

[1] These texts together form the collection of 'Palatine Laws'.

Majorca might have been able to resist him, but was hampered by the lack of support from his traditional ally France which at that time was at grips with England; it was the beginning of the Hundred Years' War. In order to counter the ambitions of the King of Aragon, James tried to ally himself with all the enemies of Peter IV. Having lost the help of France he even sought an alliance with Edward III of England, the mortal enemy of the king of France. These clumsy intrigues only served to make his isolation more complete. His quarrel with France on the question of Montpellier simply served the interests of Peter of Aragon. Relations between the two kingdoms, Aragon and Majorca, continued to deteriorate; there were several painful incidents, notably the high-handed detention of Constance, wife of the king of Majorca, by Peter of Aragon. In 1343 matters came to a head, and Peter IV led an armed expedition against the islands. In May he landed on the beaches of Paguera. The attitude of the islanders throughout this affair was a surprising one. The islands, whose economic prosperity was at its height, managed to avoid the consequences of this fratricidal war. The king of Aragon had taken the wise precaution of informing all the inhabitants that he would guarantee them all the rights and privileges granted by James the Conqueror; and the invaders met with no very determined resistance. From the moment of landing, deals were being made between the citizens of Palma and the king of Aragon, and on the 31st of May Peter was able to march into the capital without bloodshed; a few weeks later he had himself proclaimed king of Majorca. James III fled to the mainland and the struggle ended with the surrender of the castle of Bellver and Pollensa. Minorca and Ibiza were conquered at the end of 1343. James still had his possessions on the mainland; the king of Aragon decided immediately to annex them, and attacked and besieged Perpignan. James's last bastion fell, and the 'former king of Majorca' had to surrender to Peter IV under particularly humiliating conditions.

But even though completely dispossessed of his lands, James would not accept defeat. He succeeded in escaping to Puigcerda and raising a revolt of its inhabitants against the king of Aragon. He travelled to Aragon and tried, without much success, to win the Pope over to his cause. The only thing really in his favour was his large fortune, a part of which he immediately used to build an invasion fleet. After six years of exile, supported by the Genoese to whom he had promised various advantages, James put his plan into action in October 1349. He landed with a few troops in the Bay of Alcudia, took Pollensa and routed the forces of Peter IV. But the Aragonese defended themselves by a curious type of retreat; they forced the majority of the inhabitants to withdraw into the Palma region. They then sent for urgent reinforcements from the mainland. The battle between the armies took place at Lluchmayor on October 25th, and ended with the defeat and death of James. His eleven-year-old son was taken prisoner. The victor, Peter, refused even to let James's body rest in the island; he had him buried at Valencia.

The battle of Lluchmayor dealt the final blow to the kingdom of Majorca as an independent State, eighty-seven years after its creation. Only the heir to the throne was left, a boy of eleven, James IV, the circumstances of whose later life were appalling. Held captive by his uncle who had reviled, defeated and killed his father, his only thought was to escape and regain his kingdom. In 1362, with the help of the last adherents of the Majorcan royal house, James IV succeeded in escaping. But he never regained the kingdom, although he continued to plot and scheme until his death in 1375.

However, the history of the islands was by no means closely bound up with that of the royal house. True, the golden age of independence was accompanied by brilliant achievement in the fields of culture and architecture. But it can be said that in the fourteenth and fifteenth centuries the economic progress of the islands was far from being broken by their annexation to Aragon. It was at the beginning of the fifteenth century that the merchant princes began to build their palaces. At Palma, the Lonja, or Lodge, was begun in 1426 by the architect Sagrera. Last but not least, it was during this period that the Balearic Islands were at their most prosperous, and that they became a centre for geographers and cartographers, so that they played a leading part in the history of discoveries by sea.

During this latter part of the Middle Ages there was an acute shortage of precious metals which led explorers to Africa, to the almost legendary Sudan. While the activity of Venice was centred on Alexandria and her spices, Genoa concentrated her efforts on the gold of the Sudan. The gold trade was carried on along the caravan routes of the desert, ending at Oran, then the gold passed through Majorca on its way to Barcelona or Genoa. At the beginning of the fifteenth century the Balearic Islands, and especially Majorca, made considerable progress thanks to the well-equipped port of Palma, the textile works set up in the island, and the slave trade carried on by the Genoese for the merchants of Palma.

These Genoese played an important part in the life of the islands, living as they did in the capital in a colony which formed a sort of posting-house on the traditional routes of the Genoese Republic; their ships going from the Dodecanese to Flanders put in there, bringing spices, cotton and even corn from Sicily. For the better equipped vessels going to the Atlantic, Palma was an important port of call. What cargoes were taken on board at Majorca? 'A few local products such as sulphur, fruit, soap, and wool or fleeces for Genoa. But the bulk of the merchandise had been brought from Africa: gum arabic, Melegueta pepper which came across the Sahara to the ports of the Maghrib, and hundreds of loads of dates. There is even mention of ostrich feathers. We must add especially wool from Barbary, leather from Bougie, and almost certainly gold. Thus by calling at Majorca sailors avoided the ports of northern Africa.'[1] Palma was at that time a focal point for the whole of the western Mediterranean.

But the economic rise was not the whole story. It can be said that the Balearic Islands and Palma, in the same way as Pisa, Genoa and Venice, played a leading

[1] J. Heers, *Gênes au XV* siècle*, Paris 1961.

part in the cartographical revolution which, as soon as the compass came into general use, was to lead to so many great discoveries.

The birth of the Majorcan school cannot, it seems, be dissociated from certain traditions present in the Iberian peninsula. 'The geographical and cosmographical sciences are mainly of Moslem and Jewish origin, which does not mean that Christians have had nothing to do with them.'[1] Apart from this contamination by tradition, we have to take into account the nautical experience of these Aragonese seamen, permanently in touch with the Majorcans, who sailed the Atlantic waters off the coasts of Africa and Europe.

What is the state of our present knowledge of the Majorcan school of cartography?

We have a map dated 1338, made by Angelino Dulcert, consisting of two folios measuring 57 by 29½ inches, with the following colophon: '*Hoc opus fecit Angelino Dulcert MCCCXXXVIII de Mense Augusti in civitate Maioricarum*'. Little is known of its author, and it is not certain that this map, which shows the area between Spain and the Caspian Sea, is complete. Specialists say it is strongly influenced by the Italian school. We have, on the other hand, much fuller information about the Cresques family, the authors of the famous *Catalan Atlas*. We do not know the exact date of birth of Abraham Cresques, 'the most illustrious of Majorcan cartographers'; we know that about 1350 he was working for the royal house of Aragon as 'astrologer and master of maps and compasses'. His record of service and outstanding work caused him to be singled out for the king's favour. The Infante Jaime rewarded him and gave him the right to settle in Palma in a palace with bath-house (this was a favour, considering the conditions forced upon Jews at this period). Abraham had a son, Jafuda, who worked under his father at a very early age. When Abraham died in 1387 he took over his work. He escaped the great pogrom against the Majorcan Jews in 1391, but had to be converted to Christianity, taking the name of Jaume Ribes; he was forced to flee from the island and settled in Barcelona in 1394. He was then summoned by Prince Henry to the court at Lisbon, where he was known as Master James of Majorca.

Of the many maps made by Abraham and Jafuda Cresques only one remains: the *Catalan Atlas* dating from 1375-1377. It is a real universal atlas with six woodcuts, eight maps and four astronomical diagrams; according to Charles de la Roncière it is 'the prototype of the map of northern Europe as it has remained for two centuries, and the most perfect cartographic representation of India and the Far East before the arrival of the Portuguese'. The fame of this work is shown by the interest taken in it by King Charles VI of France; he sent to the king of Aragon his messenger Guillaume de Courcy, who brought the map back to Paris, where it is still kept in the Bibliothèque Nationale.

Among the great names of Majorcan cartography we may also note that of

[1] G. de Reparaz, 'Activité maritime et commerciale du royaume d'Aragon au XIII° siècle' (*Bulletin hispanique*, vol. 49, 1947).

Mecia de Villadestes (whose map, dating from 1413, is also in the Bibliothèque Nationale in Paris). The pogrom of 1391 forced the Jews who were carrying on the tradition of the Cresques family to work under Christian names: Guilermus Soleri, Petrus Rossell, Olivio, and Gabriel de Vallsecha whose map of the world, carried out in 1439, belonged to Amerigo Vespucci, and, carelessly handled by George Sand, was stained with ink in the nineteenth century. The lines of this map are excellent as far as Africa is concerned; in fact they include 'the track followed by the Citroen caterpillar-tractors which arrived in Timbuctoo in 1922'.[1] Despite the decadence noticeable from 1450 onwards, the Majorcan school did not receive its death-blow until 1492, the year when the Jews were expelled from Spain.

This summary of the questions of the Majorcan maps serves to emphasize the fact that the Balearic Islands played a leading part in the history of science, and, in fact, in that of world scholarship as a whole. They took over from the scientific studies of the Iberian peninsula, which were strongly influenced by Jewish and Arabic culture; and they heralded the discoveries made later under Henry the Navigator. Combined with the extraordinary cosmopolitan atmosphere which reigned on Majorca at the height of its political and commercial expansion, the work of the Majorcan cartographers gave the Balearic Islands a place in a far wider historical setting than that of the archipelago itself. We have seen how the complex struggles in which the islands were engaged involved them in a curious way with the history of the Iberian peninsula, Italy, the Papacy, England and above all France. The fact that the islands played a part in the history of Europe and in the discovery of the world is a particularly clear illustration of their need to remain in contact with the outside world if they are to make an important contribution. For them, the essential thing is not to be isolated. The golden age of the Balearic Islands corresponds exactly with their integration into a State which may have been still-born, but was basically no different from the kingdom of Sardinia whose part in the nineteenth century struggle for Italian unity is so well-known.

FROM THE FIFTEENTH TO THE TWENTIETH CENTURY

Once they were politically integrated in the Iberian Peninsula, the history of the islands became less brilliant. At the beginning of the fifteenth century a period of development seems to have taken place on Majorca; a large number of merchants, attracted by the island's prestige, came to settle there, contributing to the improvement of the inland areas. 'Eleven villages were built in country districts which had never before been ploughed or harrowed.'[2] The 'colonial-type' villages, with their streets intersecting at right-angles, like La Puebla, date

[1] Charles de la Roncière, *La découverte de l'Afrique au Moyan Age*, Cairo 1927.
[2] J. d'Hermilly, *Histoire du royaume de Majorque*, Maastricht 1777.

from this period. In 1436 the Majorcans took part in the conquest of the kingdom of Naples by Alfonso V of Aragon, providing galleys for the royal fleet, which shows how much their nautical traditions were still appreciated by their 'new' masters. This compulsory military service, forced on them by the Aragonese crown, had the effect of exacerbating their proud and nostalgic longing for their past greatness. A revolt broke out at Lluchmayor in 1438, but was soon crushed by the governors of Palma; in addition Majorca seems, in the middle of the fifteenth century, to have been in the throes of a social crisis born of the contrast between the prosperity of the port and the relative stagnation of the inland towns. These often violent upheavals were known as the struggles of the 'foreigners' (that is, people from outside the city) against the citizens of Palma. But the fate of the Balearic Islands, which had been sealed politically at the Battle of Lluchmayor, was sealed economically at the end of the fifteenth century when Christopher Columbus's discovery in 1492 turned the eyes of Spain towards the west.

'Until then, there was no one of any wealth in Majorca who did not possess galleys which the king of Spain frequently borrowed; those who had their own vessels enjoyed several privileges, including that of being the only ones allowed to have battlemented towers on their country houses. For this reason the Majorcans had always had a great deal of contact with foreigners. There were so many advantages to be gained from it that most of the citizen-soldiers refused to accept noble rank so that they could qualify for the Consulate, the association of merchants, and there were even nobles who for the same reason asked the king for permission to renounce their titles and become ordinary citizens; the citizens were so highly regarded that these requests were always granted. As time passed, a different way of thinking arose. The discovery of the New World may be the main reason for this. Deprived of the rich resources which trade had hitherto provided for them, the Majorcans devoted themselves almost entirely to agriculture. Thus, relinquishing the helm to take up plough and hoe, they withdrew into their island, and henceforth thought only of developing their fields and country estates.'[1]

The nautical traditions of the islands were not, however, completely forgotten. At the beginning of the sixteenth century warships appear to have been more in evidence than merchant ships, for the Mediterranean was being hard hit by the expansion of the Turkish empire. The function of the islands changed; they became a military base and the object of bitter struggles. During the whole of the sixteenth century agricultural progress in the islands was brought to a standstill by pirate raids. In 1509 and 1510 the first blow was struck against the Turks by the capture of Oran, followed by that of Bougie; a large number of ships armed at Palma took part. These marauding expeditions brought to Majorca a large number of prisoners of war, who were in effect slaves, as there was never any intention of freeing them. 'They were used in great numbers both in the

[1] *ibid.*

50

galleys and for farm-work. Well-to-do people had no other servants but slaves; practically no one else did the work of coachmen, labourers, shepherds, carters and carriers, so that they were to be feared because of both their numbers and their function, however much care the masters of Gayetta took to keep them under, punishing them severely, as was their right, for the slightest fault.'[1] Parallel with these doubtful fortunes at sea came social upheavals within the islands, known as the war of Communities or Brotherhoods (Germania) lasting from 1521 to 1523. The revolt arose from a financial quarrel about unequal taxation; it was led by a certain Juan Crespi who put Majorca to fire and sword to such an extent that the viceroy Don Miguel had to leave the island and take refuge on Ibiza for some weeks. This civil war was marked by a number of battles, notably several sieges of Alcudia.

Without going so far as to speak of a decline, it appears that around 1530 the island province suffered a certain setback caused to some extent by the pressure exerted by the pirates. From 1535 to 1541, Minorca was sacked and occupied by the famous Barbarossa. In 1541 the emperor Charles V decided to put an end to the depredations of the Algerian pirate. He collected together a fleet and put in at Palma; on October 13th he made a ceremonial visit to the town, then he put to sea, and on October 18th the squadron laid siege to Algiers. Unfortunately the attempt failed, and the emporor had no alternative but to let his enemy go on scouring the Mediterranean sea routes. In 1550 Pollensa was again besieged, by Dragut Arraez, a creature of Barbarossa. In 1552, Valldemosa was sacked, and in 1553 Andraitx, thanks to a certain Collas, fell to the attacks of the Berbers.

The memory of these different adventures is still kept alive today. In the course of many patronal festivals they are commemorated by mock battles in which, for the delight of crowds of tourists, the wicked Moor is overcome and handed over, bound hand and foot, to the Christian judgement of the king of Spain. Costumes and weapons, carefully looked after by the fishermen or the inhabitants of the ports, add to these shows a touch of local colour which is always a great draw.

In the middle of the sixteenth century the principal towns had strong walls built against the constant threat of attack. Finally, in 1571, the victory of Lepanto brought the islands the long-awaited respite, but at the same time they entered upon a period of calm during which they took no part in warlike enterprises. During the whole of the end of the sixteenth century and for more than a century after, they took their place among the dominions of Spain, acting as a stopping-place on the route between the kingdom and its possessions in Italy. The influence of Italian Renaissance and Settecento art on the way of life of the Balearic Islands began to be felt. Palaces were built on Majorca which to this day add their own charm to Palma and the surrounding countryside.

In spite of the fact that Majorcan contingents played a large part in crushing

[1] ibid.

51

the revolt of Naples in 1647, and in spite of the bombing of Palma in 1706 by an Anglo-Dutch fleet, Majorca went through history without any very spectacular shocks.

At the end of the seventeenth century the Balearic Islands were involved in the war of the Spanish Succession; like Valencia and Catalonia, they took the side of the Archduke Charles of Austria against Philip V.

In 1708 the English landed on Minorca, so that its history diverged from that of the other islands for almost a hundred years. In 1713 the treaty of Utrecht separated it from the kingdom of Spain, and it came under English influence during the whole of the first half of the century. These political ties had far-reaching consequences on the economic history of the islands. In 1738 the English engineer Armstrong published in London a most interesting book,[1] a particularly remarkable example of historical and, even more, geographical and economic analysis applied to the island. This work, written a century before that of George Sand, marks an important stage in the history of writings on the Balearic Islands, which ever since the Roman period had been the concern mainly of Catalan chroniclers and Spanish historians. Northern Europe could now begin to have some knowledge of the islands over which France and England were quarrelling after the treaty of Versailles in 1756. Minorca, which was fortified for thirty years, was at that time a strategic point as important as Gibraltar or Malta have ever been. Marshal Richelieu thought he could strike a telling blow at England by attempting to take the island, the possession of which was a guarantee of power in the Mediterranean. A French fleet consisting of twelve men-of-war, five frigates and a hundred and fifty transport vessels left the islands of Hyères on April 10, 1756. On the 17th the first landing was made at Ciudadela, but victory was bound to go to the side that could hold or storm Fort San Felipe at Port Mahon. The French squadron, commanded by the Marquis de la Galisson-ière, while Richelieu laid siege to the citadel, prevented the reinforcements under Admiral Bing from entering the port. On May 20th, battle was joined be-tween the two squadrons, ending in a victory for the French. Fort San Felipe was thus cut off, and the siege continued until June 28th, when the French troops under Marshal Richelieu took the last English positions. This episode of the war between the French and English had considerable repercussions in France. Louis XV's reception of Richelieu was scarcely enthusiastic; he could think of no better question to ask him than 'What did you think of the figs in Minorca?' A mass of literature has been written on this victory, the first French naval victory for fifty years, marking the renewal of French sea power. Voltaire wrote several pieces in honour of the Duc de Richelieu; they were followed by odes, poems, songs and writings of all kinds, taking up no less than three hundred and thirty pages of close print in a volume published in Paris in 1757.[2] Minorca

[1] John Armstrong, *The History of the Island of Minorca*, London 1752.
[2] *Recueil général des pièces, chansons et fêtes données à l'occasion de la prise de Port-Mahon, précédé du Journal historique de la conquête de Minorque*, Paris 1757.

became one of the fashionable subjects of conversation in French society under Louis XV.

The defeat of the English was followed by Bing's execution by a firing-squad. The island was governed by the Comte de Lannion for seven years. One remarkable relic of the French occupation remains: the village of San Luis, which has a church in French style with an inscription to Louis XV over the main door.

In 1763 the island was disposed of in the treaty of Paris, and thus played a part in a piece of international diplomacy which had world-wide repercussions lasting a long time, for it mainly confirmed the loss of the French possessions in America and handed back to France the Antilles, Belleisle and her five trading bases in India. We do not know exactly for what territory Minorca was exchanged, but it is amusing to think that in the eighteenth century one of the Balearic Islands was discussed in connection with one of the treaties with the most far-reaching effects on the history of Europe, America and Asia.

We may also note that five years after French sovereignty was abandoned, the Genoese sold Corsica to France. This occupation, and then acquisition of islands in the western Mediterranean may be unconnected, or they may fit in with a systematic policy on the part of Louis XV's ministers.

From 1763 to 1782 Minorca was once more in English hands, and a new town was built to protect the Port Mahon roadstead: George Town, now renamed Villa Carlos. In 1782 the Franco-Spanish took the island again, and Nelson landed there in 1798. It was not until 1802 that the treaty of Amiens finally gave the island back to Spain.

In the background of all this rivalry of the French and English over Minorca were the maritime activities of Ibiza, which cannot be passed over, since this island flourished particularly during the whole of the eighteenth century. The enemies of the Ibicencos were sometimes the Turks, sometimes the Algerians, or the French, or the English, or even rich Spanish armaments manufacturers. Ibiza took advantage of a certain relaxing of the check kept by the Spanish crown on the movements of ships, to become a city of pirates, going off in their xebecs to board their victims, like the *palikares* of the War of Greek Independence. It would be interesting to compare these Greek corsairs with their huge moustaches with such men as Calvet, Ferrer or Riquer, whose exploits are duly commemorated by an obelisk below this white city which is so close architecturally to Hydra, Santorin, and other ports of the Aegean islands.

After Napoleon's expedition to Spain and the disastrous defeat at Bailen, the tragic business of the prisoners of Cabrera threw up a barrier between France and the Balearic Islands which took a long time to fall.[1]

In the nineteenth century all the islands kept aloof from the upheavals of European history; their life was little influenced by the Carlist troubles in Spain, and their development was controlled by economic forces, In the twentieth century, thanks to Spain's foreign policy, they managed to remain neutral

[1] See notes to illustrations 13, 14, and 15, p. 74.

throughout the First World War. A few submarines took in supplies along their coasts, more or less in secret. It was not until 1936 that a great crisis, not only Spanish but international, brought the islands with a sharp jerk back into the all-absorbing present.

We know, as Hugh Thomas remarks, that from April 1936 onwards the islands were considered by General Mola as one of the bases for the uprising. Earlier attempts by the military had failed, because they had been put into operation on the mainland. This time revolution was planned to break out on the periphery, in Spanish Morocco and in the Canary and Balearic Islands, at the same time as in Spain itself.[1]

From July 18th, the islands played an important part in the course of the Civil War. The uprising took place at the appointed time in Majorca, Minorca and Ibiza. Matters went very well in Majorca; under the leadership of General Goded, the principal points were occupied in a few hours without much blood-shed. In the morning of the 19th the victorious general took off from Son Bonet for Barcelona in order to help the nationalists in their fight against the Republic. But he was taken prisoner, and compelled by force to read a message over the Republican radio. As the day was lost for the 'Movimiento' in Catalonia, we may assume, like Hugh Thomas, that the only purpose of this message was 'to restrain his followers in Majorca from sending the aid which he had earlier begged'. The principal island was in the hands of the nationalists, and on the evening of the first day of the war it was a useful pawn to hold. All went well at Ibiza too; it was conquered in one day. But on Minorca things took a different turn. General Bosch, who had proclaimed a state of siege in Port Mahon beginning on the evening of the 18th was trapped in his own fortress by the combined forces of the Popular Front and certain elements of the garrison.[2] After two days of fighting the besieged forces had to surrender to the Republicans who thus held a trump card, the important naval base of Port Mahon. In a conflict which on several occasions almost turned into a general European war, Minorca and Majorca were by no means unimportant. The Republican government realized this, for when the situation had somewhat clarified on the mainland, they decided on an attempt to regain Majorca in August 1936. On the 9th, the Republicans put an Air Force captain named Bayo at the head of an expeditionary force made up of Catalans and Valencians embarked in four troopships escorted by the battleship *Jaime Primero*, two destroyers, two submarines and six aircraft. This fleet went first to Ibiza where there had been an anti-nationalist rising, and the island came back to the Republic. On August 13th, Bayo's expeditionary force, intoxicated by its first success, sailed along the western coast of Majorca and, judging it to be too strongly fortified, turned eastwards. At dawn on August 16th, 10,000 men landed in the creeks on the coast near Porto Cristo, which they took, forming a bridge-head about ten miles long and

[1] Hugh Thomas, *The Spanish Civil War*, London 1961.
[2] *ibid.*

54

about six deep. The nationalists counter-attacked, and with the help of Italian airmen, drove the invaders back to the sea after battles lasting until September 3rd.[1]

After Bayo's defeat, the island of Majorca, which had been spared the horrors of war, was sifted from end to end. This purge lasted from September to November and seems to have been supervised by the leader of the Italian volunteers, Count Arconovaldo Bonaccorsi, better known, thanks to the writings of Bernanos[2], under the name of Count Rossi. He and his soldiers helped the nationalists to retake Ibiza and Formentera, so that by the end of 1936 the Republicans had lost three islands. They kept Minorca, thanks to an agreement signed by England and Italy at the beginning of 1937, by which the Italian soldiers were forbidden to land there. To say the least of it, the situation was an explosive one, and on several occasions threatened to degenerate into a general war. The most serious incident was the affair of the battleship *Deutschland* on May 19, 1937. This modern ship of Hitler's fleet was 'by chance' lying at anchor in the Ibiza roadstead, when she was the object of a surprise attack at nightfall by two Republican aircraft which dropped two bombs, killing twenty-two men and wounding eighty-three. It appears to have been an isolated raid, not an operation planned by the Republican general staff. But reprisals followed immediately. The vessel got under way and was joined by four German destroyers; then at dawn on the 31st, the civil population of Almeria was mercilessly bombarded. This affair caused very seriously international tension, and the Second World War might well have started two years ealier than it did, all because of an isolated incident taking place at Ibiza in the Balearic Islands. This fact, coupled with the attacks of 'ghost submarines' led to the conference of Nyons in the course of which an attempt was made to settle the problems of the western Mediterranean (September 1937).

The Balearic Islands were once more plunged into the midst of international problems, and their earlier fame was not renewed until the moment when the Republican government was in its death-agony and the nationalists victorious. General Franco finished the conquest of Catalonia on February 10, 1939, and on the same day Minorca capitulated in very curious circumstances.

Just before his victory at Barcelona, the 'generalisimo' had made up his mind

---

[1] cf. Georges Oudart, *Chemins noires, brunes et vertes en Espagne*. Paris. 1938. This work, which is very favourable to the nationalists, gives all the details of this expedition.

[2] *Les grands Cimetières sous la Lune*, Paris 1938.

Georges Bernanos had been in Majorca since October 1934. He lived in Palma, in the street called San Catleret, then at 95 and 111 Calle del 14 Abril, and finally at 30 Calle de la Salud. His 'Majorcan' writings include the completion of *Monsieur Ouine*, *Un Mauvais Rêve* and *Un Crime*. In December 1934 he began *Le Journal d'un Curé de Campagne* and *La Nouvelle Histoire de Mouchette*. When the Civil War broke out, he was at first attracted by the ideals of the 'Movimiento'. He left Palma on March 27, 1937. The original manuscript of *Les Grands Cimetières sous la Lune* was lost. He rewrote it on returning to France (cf. A. Béguin, *Bernanos par lui-même*, Paris 1954).

to dispose finally of the 'Red Island', and informed the English government of his intention to take over the island without the help of Germans or Italians. The first contact between London and Burgos was made by Captain Hillgarth, British consul on Majorca. England's aim was apparently to impede Mussolini's designs on the islands, which he would have liked to appropriate as 'recompense' for having sent volunteers. The Foreign Office authorized a ship, the *Devonshire*, to carry Franco's negotiators from Palma to Port Mahon on condition that neither Germany nor Italy should be informed of the negotiations and that the island should be banned for two years to volunteers of the Condor Legion as well as to the Italians. Franco's men came to an agreement with the Republicans in the presence of the English commandant of the *Devonshire*, then, when matters were settled, the vessel left for Marseilles with 450 Minorcans who were particularly closely involved with the Republican government. Thus, in February 1939, the Republic's last bastion in the Balearic Islands fell, and the circumstances of its surrender were probably not without influence on the last struggles of the Valencia government; Minorca was the proof that the fight could end with honour for the vanquished.

When the dreadful episode of the Civil War was over, it was possible to realize the importance of the part the Balearic Islands played in the struggle, not only on the Spanish level, but on that of all Europe. At the same time it is not without interest to remind our readers once more that Bernanos wrote his *Grands Cimetières sous la Lune* in the Balearic Islands, and that a large section of the French-speaking intelligentsia was shaken by this warning cry.

After the Civil War, the Balearic Islands went through a period of recession. The European war meant the loss of the tourists who had begun to know and love them.

Then came the slow healing of the wounds received in the struggles, and the almost fairy-tale awakening of the islands as the tourists began to visit them once more.

These centuries of history seem to pervade every corner, however remote. What tales we might hear from the white chapels of Ibiza, the red earth of Santa Ponsa, the arcades of Ciudadela, the gates of Alcudia, the rocks of Cabrera, the beaches of Manacor – if they could speak!

Chapter IV

THE END OF ISOLATION

ONE of the most striking features of the human geography of the Balearic Islands is that despite the eternal presence of the sea they are islands of peasants, landowners and townsmen rather than fishermen (with the exception of Formentera). With a population of 441,842 on December 31, 1958, they have less than 5,000 fishermen. If we try to compare these islands with the other Spanish provinces, we realize that there is not one genuine fishing port. Palma (only as far as fishing is concerned) comes 58th among Spanish ports.[1] Another characteristic of the way of life of these islanders is the importance of the towns. On July 1, 1960, Palma had 162,000 inhabitants, making it one of the twelve largest towns in Spain; there are eight conurbations of more than 10,000 inhabitants scattered over the three main islands.[2] They are fairly densely populated areas, as the density per square mile is 217.56 inhabitants (as against 143.51 on the mainland). This great importance given to towns can be recognized as one of the common characteristics of Mediterranean life. The inhabitants of the Balearic Islands seem to avoid the shores, which were for a long time sources of danger, and to gather in dense urban centres where the houses are crowded together and, on the coast, often protected by surrounding walls. Such are the little Majorcan towns of Selva, Pollensa, and especially Alcudia; such are the ports of Minorca like Port Mahon and Ciudadela; and even the great city of Ibiza. In the not-so-remote times when these cities were self-supporting, the concentration of dwellings made it necessary for farmers to live at some distance from their land. Every morning at sunrise, light carts drawn by a donkey or a mule drive along the roads leading out of the villages; they are loaded with agricultural tools, even a little plough. The owner of a small plot may have an hour's journey to reach it, returning at night worn out and irritable. Around the towns of Pollensa, Alcudia and La Puebla, whole families are sometimes seen coming back from the fields on summer evenings. The father holds the reins, and the mother and children are beside him. Even at the beginning of the century the geographer Jean Brunhes had been struck by this sight:[3] 'For five or six hours I followed

---

[1] This trait can be attributed to persistent traces of the Arab occupation.

[2] These are, in descending order of size: Manacor, Port Mahon, Inca, Ibiza, Felanitx, Ciudadela, La Puebla, and Lluchmayor.

[3] Jean Brunhes, *Revue des Deux Mondes*, 1st Nov. 1911.

a bad road; it was a charming lane between the olive-trees. I decided to count the carts following each other in procession as they returned from the fields, and I passed ninety-seven of them. Their loads were delightful. . . .'

The only difference in the last fifty years is that this procession of travellers is now completed by starved-looking cyclists, riding along with straw hats on their heads, their blue cotton shirts billowing in the wind, a wooden fork tied to the frame of their bicycle, often accompanied by a dog. Often all these vehicles drive along without a thought for those newcomers to their domain, the motorists. They have no lights to mark their position, and tourists driving at night are haunted by the fear of causing an accident. These twice-daily migrations have sometimes other consequences; the mules' or donkeys' shoes leave deep prints in the tar of the roads, and, what is more, innumerable nails resulting in frequent punctures.

The Balearic Islands are inhabited mainly by farmers living in concentrated groups of dwellings around the sources of water. But as the type of country varies, so do the crops grown by the people; it is the natural result of that diversity of landscape in which tourists take such delight.

Of the 1,935 square miles of land covered by the archipelago, more than half is cultivated.

The types of crop found on Majorca differ, naturally enough, according to the regions. Thus in the mountainous area of the Great Sierra and in the north-eastern region of Arta, the principal crops are the olive and the carob-bean, except in the Soller basin where citrus fruits grow in quantity, and except at Bañalbufar and Estellenchs where there are terraces similar to those found in China; these terraces consist of elongated rectangles about three metres wide, forming steps going right down to the sea. The landscape, patterned with these steps, takes on the red-brown colour of the fertile soil of the gardens. 'I have never encountered a specimen of the Mediterranean style of agriculture on irrigated terraces, so apparently perfect as the terraces of Bañalbufar' wrote Jean Brunhes.[1]

In the central plain, around Sineu, San Juan, Maria de la Salud, Petra, Villafranca and Manacor, lies an area where almonds, cereal crops and vegetables grow easily. The fertile ground makes it possible to grow crops without irrigation in clay soils with a deep layer of topsoil.

In the south-west, around Lluchmayor, Porreras and Felanitx, the soil is less rich and the topsoil not so deep, and there is less water; here there are fig and almond trees in quantity. Cereals and vegetables are grown in rotation. The most productive part of the island is the well-watered and well-tended area of the *huertas* around La Puebla, Muro, Palma (the region of Prat de San Jordi) and Campos del Puerto. For visitors the chief features of this region are the *norias*, similar to those of the Maghrib, which are tending to be replaced by windpumps in irrigating the crops with the help of underground water. Agriculture

[1] *ibid.*

58

here is an industry (although the excessive cutting up of the land into small plots is a hindrance) and this region produces the best returns. Wheat, potatoes, French beans, cotton, tobacco, and broad beans grow in abundance. The whole island lives on this region, to such an extent that during the Civil War, at a time when Majorca was completely cut off from the mainland, the inhabitants could subsist without suffering the stringent rationing of their other compatriots; and this, incidentally, was not without influence on the fortunes of certain land-owners. In various parts of Majorca especially in the deeply undulated regions or on the spurs of the Sierra, there are a few herds of goats, sheep, or black pigs like those of Ulysses. Vines are everywhere; and a few acres here and there around the villages can make possible the production of some very famous wines such as those of Inca and more especially those of Binisalem and Felanitx. They mature in huge wooden vats; they are highly appreciated and as good as some of the great wines of the mainland. They have an alcoholic content of up to 16°, and a delicate aroma, full of sunshine. The vineyards, except for those around Felanitx, produce mainly red wine.

On Minorca the physical features and, even more, the direction of the winds, necessitate quite a different type of cultivation. The island is a kind of limestone plateau, isolated in the middle of the Mediterranean, with both ends split into deep clefts containing the two harbour towns of Port Mahon and Ciudadela which have more than half the population between them. 'There is not much soil, but it is good', say the peasants. It is a thin layer lying in the hollows of the core of limestone rock. However, as men planted the ground, they took out the stones, which, as they accumulated, formed the sort of wall, one or two metres high, which gives the Minorcan landscape its peculiar character. These 'ramparts' also protect against the wind, particularly the north wind or tramontana, which blows on an average for a hundred and twenty days a year and determines the climate of the island and thus its agriculture. There are few trees. In the north herbaceous and fodder plants are grown, particularly sainfoin which is the basic food of their most important type of livestock. On Minorca, in fact, the majority of farmers breed cattle, which is surprising, and quite exceptional in the Mediterranean. Herds of cows, black and white like those of Brittany, are the main wealth of the inhabitants; the country districts live on the dairy industry, notably the production of 'queso de Mahon' or Minorcan cheese, which is famed throughout the islands, and in the towns the animals' hides are used in the shoe factories. The southern region is much less fertile, as the layer of soil is thinner. Except for the two ends of the island, where farming is carried on in irrigated fields, Minorca uses mainly a type of non-irrigated farming based on triennial rotation.

On Ibiza, where, incidentally, the influence of the sea is more important than on the other islands – as is shown by the activities of the population at the present day and still more in the past – the economy is predominantly a peasant one, based on the country and on farming. A little of everything is grown, and no region is devoted specifically to one crop. The rather haphazard distribution of the hills make it impossible to draw a clear distinction between contrasting regions; we find a coastal plain around the principal town, another around San Antonio Abad and a third around Santa Eulalia. Here, growers raise mixed crops in small fragmented plots – potatoes, melons, strawberries. On land where irrigation is not possible, such as the hillsides, almonds, a little wheat, broad beans, vetches and figs are grown. There are a large number of pine forests, so that there is some profit to be made from forestry. It is an island of landowners, grouped in large villages; the separation between country folk and townsfolk is particularly noticeable. There are the people of Ibiza – that is, the town itself, the port – who turn by tradition towards the sea, and there are the people who live in the country.

Opposite Ibiza, and less than half an hour from the port, is Formentera, a barren island by contrast with its relatively fertile neighbour. The inhabitants of Formentera cannot be self-supporting. It is to the Mediterranean what the Ile de Sein is to Brittany. This narrow tongue of flat land buffeted by the wind is formed of rocky ground which, rather like Minorca, can be cultivated only in small plots with a thin layer of topsoil. Some Cereals and vegetable crops are grown, and there are a few herds of goats. The major resources of the island are fishing, the salt pans around San Francisco, and now the tourist industry.

The sight of these farming activities, which seem very anachronistic to most visitors, may tend to make us think that they are thousands of years old. But it would appear that this face which the islands show to us as soon as we leave the towns and villages is not nearly as ancient as some traditions would have us believe. There are certain particular moments when history brings about fundamental alterations in the economic activity of a country. An article by Juliette-Pierre Monbeig[1] gives us a masterly view of a complete change in the dominant characteristics of the agriculture of the Balearic Islands which was brought about only two hundred years ago, in the eighteenth century. It was an English governor, Sir Richard Kane, whose administration completely transformed Minorcan agriculture while he was in office (1726-1736). The peasants took advantage of the general feeling of security stemming from the protection which the English fleet gave to the coasts, and were able to spend more time removing stones from their fields, making their hedges, and planting wind-barriers. It appears that the very characteristic Minorca landscape goes no further back than this period. Living conditions in the island were modified, and there was even a population explosion, rising from 16,082 inhabitants in 1723 to 20,815 in 1749. In this land, buffeted by the north wind, scarcely protected by its low hills, the traditional crop was that of cereals, but in the colonial period new ones were added, such as potatoes, grapes, and clover. The building of the road from Mahon to Cuidadela (1713-1720) provided a means of communication right across the island, and opened the way to trade in agricultural products.

It was foreign influence that changed Minorcan economy, but on Majorca

[1] 'La Real Sociedad de los Amigos del Pais'. Annales du Midi, vol. 45, Paris 1933.

and Ibiza the transformation was due to other factors and happened a little later. 'Until about 1775 the economic situation in the islands remained what it had been since the end of the fifteenth century; the land was self-supporting, thanks rather to good natural conditions than to the work of the inhabitants.'[1] The revolution which transformed the landscape was a psychological one. In 1778 a society was formed of people of high rank, called the *Sociedad Economica de los Amigos del Pais*; its activities were centred on Palma, mainly because its brochures were published there. The ambition of these 'Majorcan physiocrats' was to clear all uncultivated land, to assist the development of the growing of crops, trees, and vines, to develop stock-rearing by the introduction of artificial meadows, and to cultivate textile plants such as flax and hemp to supply local looms. Within a few years the right psychological climate for the modernization of the traditional institutions of the islands were created through the influence of French aristocrats and priests fleeing from the Revolution. The arrival of Napoleon's troops in Catalonia caused a complete exodus towards Palma; in 1811 there were 40,000 refugees in Majorca. Something new was happening in the islands. In the field of agriculture, the period 1750-1850 saw a spectacular change: 'The large properties devoted to cereals gave way to orchards of much smaller size.'[2] In the first half of the century almond trees were systematically planted in the flat region. Thus the economic structure of all the islands has changed since the eighteenth century; and the resulting type of agriculture is still lively and effective today and forms the basis of the islands' wealth. Other branches of activity in the Balearic islands have, until the last few years, remained as static as agriculture was progressive. We cannot of course study here in detail all the aspects of industry and crafts in the Balearic Islands; we shall confine ourselves to a few notes on the principal trades of the inhabitants. Traditionally, the oldest industry is that of salt, carried on mainly on Ibiza and Formentera, and around the bay of Alcudia in Majorca.

Then comes the lignite mining industry located mainly on Majorca (Alaro and Llosetta). The greatest activity is in the textile industry; towns like Soller and Inca are centres where weaving is carried on in either cotton or wool. Before the period of industrialization tapestry and weaving were flourishing crafts, and some workshops, such as the one run by M. Vicens in Pollensa, are today attempting to revive a fine tradition.

The canning industry is a profitable one for firms producing tins of apricot pulp, tomatoes, and young vegetables. The meat-producing industry with its centres at Felanitx, Manacor and Soller makes canned meat, and, above all, sausages of various kinds, some of which are justly famous. A few distilleries produce anis (Santa Maria), liqueurs (Majorca and Ibiza) and gin (Minorca, with its English tradition). But one industry flourishes above all others – that of leather goods and footwear. On Majorca alone there are more than six thousand workers in the industry and sixty factories, producing more than four million pairs of

[1] *ibid.*   [2] *ibid.*

shoes a year. In this island the work is mass-produced and mainly supplies military boots for the quarter-master's department. In Minorca the work is finer and more of a craftsman's job; much of it is made to measure. We may complete this rapid survey of the economic activity of the islands by mentioning that every town and village has its weaver and its cabinet-maker who makes wooden furniture of all kinds including chairs and tables; and by adding that there are two more particularly lively industries – pearls and glassware.

Artificial pearls are made on Majorca, mainly in Manacor. This industry is of recent origin, going back to 1932, the year in which two manufacturers from Cyonnax set up a factory there for making combs and celluloid articles. At present the principal firm is the Industria Española de Perlas Imitacion, employing more than seven hundred women workers. The founder of this firm, a Frenchman who took Spanish nationality, was able to make particularly rapid progress thanks to the Civil War. The traditional sources of supply, Japan, Czechoslovakia and France, dried up as a result of the 1936-1939 emergency, and gradually, helped by the advantages of naturally gifted workers, this factory has become one of the chief ones in Spain, and is at present extending its activities to certain European markets.

The glass industry is older and more traditional. It was introduced by the Carthaginians, the descendants of the Phoenicians, between the fourth and third centuries B.C., as proved by various objects to be seen in the museums of Alcudia and Arta. Traditional shapes and manufacturing techniques have lasted through Roman, Arab and Christian civilizations and are still in use today. However, the history of Majorcan glassware is inseparable from the period when the kingdom was independent. In 1347, in the reign of Peter IV of Aragon, a Catalan crafts-man, Guillermo Barcelo, came to settle in Majorca and obtained permission to set up a kiln. At that period the fear of deforestation was so strong in the island – for wood was practically the only source of energy – that royal permission was needed to set up a new kiln; and even then, the daily consumption of wood was strictly limited. After the first impetus had been given by the Catalan artist, the monopoly of glass manufacture passed to a craftsman called Nicolas Colonna, who from 1398 onwards was able to make a variety of articles at unrivalled prices. From the fourteenth to the eighteenth century was the golden age of the Balearic glassmakers. They produced intricately decorated bottles, flagons, jars and cups, a few rare specimens of which are still to be found. In the seventeenth century, in 1605, certain particular political circumstances obliged a Venetian, Domenico Barrionieri, exiled from his native country, to take refuge in Majorca. He gave Majorcan craftsmanship its second wind by bringing with him the secrets of the Venetian art of glassmaking. In the eighteenth century it was Germans who perfected the technique. Today only a few firms remain to inherit a tradition almost a thousand years old. Two are of particular interest to visitors; one is in the village of Campanet, and the other, Gordiola, is near the walls in Palma.

Apart from these two sectors, artificial pearls and glassware, it is difficult to find any signs of modernity in any of the islands' activities except in the newest of all – the tourist industry.

Improvements in transport would certainly have enabled many tourists to share the beauties of the islands, but the basic services necessary to accommodate them were lacking for a long time.

As far as transport within the islands is concerned, the first serious attempt was made by the railways, and that only in Majorca. In 1875 the first line was opened, from Palma to Inca, 18 miles long. Little by little, a remarkable network, for the period, was built up; 134 miles of line linking the principal towns with Palma. It was a narrow gauge line, it is true, but until the thirties it was the only link between the interior of the island and the capital. Development is still continuing today; the trains are now all drawn by diesel engines. A line which has been electrified since 1928 links Palma and Soller; it is as beautiful a run as any in Switzerland, and with its numerous viaducts and tunnels forms an artistic and admirable example of railways building in mountainous country.

During the thirties, the motor car gradually replaced the railway as a means of reaching the interior of the island. But for too long a time the roads were nothing but dusty lanes, transforming the smallest vehicle going at more than 12 miles an hour into a sort of rocket trailing a vast white plume of dust. Nowadays all the roads are asphalted, but only at the cost of sustained effort; results showed only a little at a time, with such achievements as the building of double carriage-ways, and the mapping out of new routes such as the remarkable road linking Andraitx and Estellenchs, or the very recent one between Soller and Lluch, built to satisfy not only the tourists but the Army (there is in fact a military base in the massif of Puig Mayor). These days the tourists, who are invariably in a hurry, have absolutely no idea of the effort which has gone into this network of roads. And yet how much we owe to these nameless roadmen! They are thin and Don Quixote-like, with their great tropical-looking straw hats in which they could be taken for convicts; the blue cotton shirts they wear in summer hang out over the trousers which are tied up with string. They work continuously, like ants, carrying earth for the embankment, and even pieces of rock in their inadequate little wicker baskets.

It need not concern us here whether the motor car has created the modern road or the modern road the car; however the weight of traffic on the roads is determined by the ease with which fuel can be obtained. If we were to write a complete history of the tourist industry in the Balearic Islands, we would probably discover that the density of traffic depends on the number of filling-stations for petrol or diesel-oil.

Parallel with this rapid progress in communications came what we might almost call a revolution in sources of power. It is hard to say at exactly what date electricity was introduced into the islands. We can, however, say that at the beginning of the twentieth century all the principal villages were equipped

63

with small steam-generating stations fed mainly with wood or almond shells (a fuel, incidentally, which is commonly used by the inhabitants). About 1927, larger companies began to be formed in an attempt to co-ordinate this rather haphazard whole. The ravages of the Civil War were felt here too, and it was not until 1946 that a small power station was built at Palma. But as far as Majorca is concerned it was not until 1956 that a plan took shape to install a plant capable of supplying the demand for power of the whole island, and the great power-station at Alcudia was built. Today it disfigures one of the most beautiful bays, but it was built there in response to urgent and definite needs; for instance it had to be near a refuelling station for oil tankers. It is supplied with fuel both by the island's lignite mines and by a coaster which calls once a month. Minorca and Ibiza were quick to follow the example of Majorca, and they too have modern power-stations providing electricity for the inhabitants and . . . for the tourists.

Just as important as these achievements in the fields of transport and power is the question of the provision of hotels and the development of such means of access as ports and airports. All these heavy investments are now paying dividends, simply because for more than a hundred years the Balearic Islands have been basking in the sun of a successful tourist industry.

The Balearic Islands first made their mark in France during the period of the French Revolution. François Arago, sent to the islands on a scientific mission to measure the length of the meridian, left a picturesque account of his stay in Majorca.[1] Then came the tragic story of the French soldiers imprisoned at Cabrera[2] after the disaster of Bailen, which aroused considerable interest. The writings of Corporal Wagré,[3] for example did much to preserve the memory of the appalling conditions of their imprisonment.[4] It is easy to understand the far-reaching effects of these writings if we compare them with all those which forged the 'Emperor-cult' in France during the first half of the nineteenth century.

In 1838-1839, Chopin's illness brought George Sand to Majorca, and gave rise to her – not always favourable – account in *Un hiver a Majorque*. Chopin was in fact ill and seeking a refuge; and the winter of 1838-1839 was cold and rainy. The couple, once installed in a cell in the monastery of Valldemosa, began to be talked about in the village; neither George Sand nor Chopin was ever seen in church, and George Sand's daughter wore trousers. While they waited for the piano that had been ordered,[5] boredom reigned in the clammy cold of the monastery, despite the kindness of their hosts. At night, George Sand was wakened by the squealing of pigs. One day she even found fleas on a roast

---

[1] *Histoire de ma jeunesse*, Leipzig 1854.
[2] cf. Geisendorf des Gouttes, *Les Archipels enchanteurs et farouches*, Geneva 1937.
[3] Wagré, *Souvenirs d'un caporal de grenadiers*, Paris 1902.
[4] cf. notes to illustrations 13, 14, and 15, p. 74.
[5] cf. notes to illustrations 30 and 31, p. 76.

chicken. That was enough to make her pour forth bitter reflections on the vulgarity and spitefulness of the Majorcans. 'But to tell the truth, she gives us no real evidence of it. The good lady reminds us on this point of the wives of civil servants who declare: "You can't imagine what a spiteful lot they are at St Quentin!".'[1]

Majorca, then, is the island which first appeals to the curiosity of foreigners, particularly the mountainous part around Valldemosa, Miramar and Deya. In 1867 there arrived in the island a certain Count von Neudorf, a brilliant, mysterious character, who returned in 1876 under his real name: His Imperial Highness the Archduke Louis Salvador of Austria, Habsburg, Lorraine and Bourbon (1847-1915). Having cruised around all the Mediterranean waters in his yacht *Nixe*, he preferred the Majorcan coast to that of Corfu, Crete or Sardinia. The charm of the island won his heart, and he set himself to study it in all its aspects. His work in nine volumes, with the title *Balearen in Wort und Bild*[2] touches upon every subject – prehistory, history, folklore, geography – and today is still the standard work on the subject. The Archduke built the great house of Son Marroig near Miramar, where he welcomed many illustrious guests: Santiago Rusiñol, Miguel de Unamuno, the Nicaraguan poet Ruben Darico, Prince Vladimir of Russia, the Empress of Austria, the Duke of Orleans. Scholars too were among his guests: the geologist Martel who studied the caves of Majorca, and botanists and ornithologists who all contributed to the study of the island. Louis Codet, who was one of his guests from France, left a rather harsh portrait of him in his *Images de Majorque*. All through his life, this passionate enthusiast had only one aim, to teach others to know and love the Balearic Islands.

After the Archduke's work appeared that of Santiago Rusiñol: *La Isla de la Calma*[3] which deals only with the largest island. Then other rich tourists came, writers, or painters, like Erwin Hubert who left a large number of landscapes of all parts of the island.

All this was bound to have its effect. Tourists were already flocking to the island, and in order to receive important guests, the first hotel worthy of the name, the Grand Hotel, was built in 1909 on the initiative of the Marquis de la Torre. In 1905 a group of 'lovers of Majorca' founded the Fomento del Turismo, which was the first institution of this type to be created in Spain.

But the man who really created the tourist industry on the grand scale in Majorca and in the Balearic Islands in general was Adam Diehl. This immensely wealthy South American bought the whole of the Formentor peninsula and in 1910 built the Hotel Formentor, intended to receive top personalities in politics, literature and the cinema. With the help of a splendidly organized publicity campaign covering the whole of Europe, he was able to count among his guests Winston Churchill, the Aga Khan, the Duke of Windsor and Douglas

[1] Louis Codet, *Images de Majorque*, Paris 1928.
[2] Leipzig, 1869-1891.   [3] Barcelona, 1913.

E   65

Fairbanks. It was one of the first luxury hotels in the world – and it was in Majorca.

Then came the Civil War and its consequences, and the tourist industry, which had reached such heights, crashed again to the ground. It was not until the fifties that reorganization was possible. Work began in earnest on the necessary facilities for tourists, the jetties at Palma were lengthened, a modern airport to take jets was built, and suitable runways were added on Minorca and Ibiza. The result is well-known and borne out by statistics; for instance the Palma airport is the second in Spain for local passenger traffic (more than a million a year – as many as Geneva).

Each year, over a period of months, a regular flood of tourists lands by boat and plane.[1] This influx, one of the densest in western Europe, is rather unusual in character. Even in comparison with Spain, visitors to the Balearic Islands are distributed in a very characteristic way. On the mainland, in fact, the French predominate; being near neighbours, they come because the cost of living is low. Out of 1,000 tourists visiting Spain, 540 are French. In the islands it is a different matter, they come from further afield. In 1964, out of 1,000 foreign tourists, there were 245 English, 175 Germans, 111 Scandinavians and 98 French. Not only do they come from further afield; they come outside the normal peak period of July and August (many English, for example, come in spring). Majorca especially benefits from this influx; out of every thousand people arriving in the islands, 881 go to Majorca, 100 to Ibiza, sixteen to Minorca and three to Formentera. (These figures can be compared with those relating to the areas of the different islands cf. p. 24.) Another significant characteristic of this type of tourism is that it is generally collective; the Palma aerodrome gives us quite a revealing insight on this point. We do of course see on the planes calling there the famous names of the great airlines, but we also see the less familiar names of a large number of companies of lesser importance. The tendency is growing to come to the Balearic Islands by charter plane. In 1964, for instance, out of a total of 1,636,821 passengers (arrivals and departures) paying the airport tax at Palma San Juan, Spanish airlines had transported 520,383 people (in both directions) thus carrying the heaviest amount of local traffic, while the share of charter planes had risen to 797,381. (The Iberia and Aviaco companies carry traffic mainly from Barcelona, and the number of Spaniards included in these statistics is considerable.) Since 1961 charter plane journeys have become increasingly popular. The groups thus formed are recruited by tourist agencies in the different urban centres of western Europe.

Despite the rise in air traffic, sea travel still plays a very important part; more than 600,000 passengers arrive at and depart from the port of Palma every year. New facilities for the transport of tourists' cars are constantly on the increase. Special airline services leave Barcelona and Nimes, making the car a sort of

[1] On this subject see M. Duchary, *Tourisme et transports en Méditerranée occidentale: Baléares, Corse, Sardaigne*. Paris 1964.

'luggage travelling with the passenger'. On the sea routes, car-ferries like the *Victoria* come to Palma from Catalonia, and very soon from Marseilles also.

Most people stay in hotels, taking a room generally for a fortnight. The Spanish government has helped considerably in the building of these hotels; in 1964 loans were made for this purpose amounting to 121.5 million pesetas (about £¾m.). Most often people stay in the Bay of Palma. There are more than 1,100 hotels in the islands, out of which 300 are near the capital and more than three-quarters are on Majorca. Prices are very reasonable; it has been calculated, for example, that a German tourist coming from Dusseldorf and spending two weeks in a good hotel on the bay of Alcudia – providing, of course that he came with a party and travelled by charter plane – would spend a total amount no greater than the cost of one normal return ticket from Dusseldorf to Palma by Lufthansa.

Although these tourists travel in parties, they do so in a different way from those who descend on the other Mediterranean islands. The tourist industry here is not based on the club, as it is in Corsica, Sardinia, Corfu or Djerba. Whereas in the other islands the club exists as a kind of enclosure where people of the same nationality live in complete separation from the outside world, keeping their own habits and customs, the tourists who come to the Balearic Islands have up to now been drawn into the life of the islands as far as was possible. This fact could be explained by the Spanish government's anxiety to keep a check on what is happening, but this would be to give too narrowly political an explanation. It can be seen rather as a very Spanish reaction – the impulse to protect an ancient civilized and well-ordered society. It is all very well to live on the tourists, as the islands once lived on trade by sea; but they refuse to let themselves be invaded, or, we might almost say, taken over. Every effort is made to keep a firm hand on the newcomers. This is still possible at present, since the foundations of this civilization have not as yet been undermined. However tolerant or indulgent the islander may feel towards his guests, they must not shock him by unseemly behaviour; too much expanse of bare legs anywhere but on the beach, and too much disturbance of the peace at night are not to be borne. This does not mean that a tourist's life is to be restricted. If the limits of propriety are exceeded, no one even mentions it to the culprit. No – the question is simply one of good manners. The Majorcan is sufficiently aware of his own worth to expect this from his guests, whom he welcomes in a way that few others can.

This sudden emergence of the Balearic Islands has naturally had far-reaching effects on their appearance. The cars on the roads are different. Until the sixties we saw a procession of old wrecks, mainly specimens of makes which no longer exist, such as Donnet, Licorne, Dion-Bouton, and old American types of car. Nowadays they have been replaced by cars made in Spain, especially Seat 600's. Modern lorries, Barreiros and Pegasos, have similarly taken over from the old ones, some of which were thirty years old.

Various commercial enterprises are developing, especially for the benefit of the tourists: travel agencies, airline companies, dealers in leather goods, foot-wear, or leather garments, jewellers' shops selling imitation pearls, shops selling folk-records, antique shops offering reproductions of stone carvings or wooden statuettes, cafes, various restaurants on the model of the German beer-cellar, English tea-rooms, Scadinavian pastry-cooks, where the most home-loving tourists can get their own national dishes. We should also mention the innumerable night-clubs run by the tourist agencies, which advertise displays of Majorcan or Spanish folk-dancing and folk-singing, usually in the open air. But the most essential element of commercial progress nowadays is either the hotel or the block of flats.

New buildings are spreading over the landscape, sometimes in record time; it is not unusual for a site to be unrecognizable from one year to the next. At Portals Vells on the Bay of Palma, expansion has been so rapid that the roads were built before the houses. The builders began with country lanes, still in bad condition, then, suddenly, there were wide roads edged with pavements, waiting for the houses to go up.

Undoubtedly the number of tourists has to depend on the facilities for receiving them. And so hundreds of new buildings are taking shape, often of fairly light materials such as hollow bricks, and covering all the various fashionable spots. The tourist industry is giving birth to what is in fact a new urban develop-ment, intended both for leisure and – it must be faced – for speculation. Among the most spectacular of the completed projects on Majorca are Magaluf on the bay of Palma and Ciudad Blanca on the bay of Alcudia. The only possible obstacles to this expansion are of course the price of land, which has increased tenfold within the space of four years, and also the problems of water supply. We must not in fact forget that this is a Mediterranean country where the rain-fall is not sufficient to satisfy more than a limited demand for water. Where there are no springs or underground water-levels, water is brought to an increas-ing extent by lorries similar to those we see carrying petrol at home. There are world famous hotels which can only subsist thanks to a cistern in the hills above them which these vehicles regularly fill.

The beaches themselves are covered with straw sunshades, giving the place an exotic appearance. To deal with the influx of tourists, more and more workers are needed. First of all the hotels have to be built, by masons, labourers and carpenters; then they have to be run, by staff who come mainly from the Malaga region of southern Spain, attracted by relatively high wages. Thus the flow of purely tourist passengers from Europe to the Balearic Islands is augmented by a seasonal migration of labour from Spain to the islands. There is also a steady flow of goods traffic; the white steamships of the *Trasmediterranea* company come to the islands loaded with tourists, but they also have their holds full of baths, taps, and other equipment which cannot be manufactured at Palma or Mahon.

Finally, this tourist boom shows itself in rocketing prices which make certain towns in the Balearic Islands the most expensive in Spain. Of course the rising standard of living has advantages for everyone, but particularly for those who began with capital to invest. In this way a balance of long standing is being tipped violently to one side.

Up to the present, since the days when the pirates used to terrify the shore-dwellers into flight, the islanders had always regarded the sea with a certain amount of caution. Palma was in a position to build strong fortifications, and the coast villages were not in general built by the sea, but two or three miles inland from the port properly speaking. Thus Andraitx, Alcudia and Pollensa, for example, were double towns: a *puerto* and a *pueblo* joined by a road, rather like Athens and the Piraeus. Until the last few years, the town proper was the centre of commercial life, while the port merely vegetated. About ten years ago the position was reversed, and now it is the port which counts, attracting tourists and building hotels, while the town falls back on its traditional activities of industry and agriculture. In ten years a situation almost a thousand years old has ended, thanks to the tourist industry. This tendency will probably strengthen as time goes on, but this spectacular rise in profits – some of which are enormous – rests in the first analysis on rather shaky foundations. We get the impression that two styles of life, one very modern and the result of the tourist industry, and the other traditional and relatively archaic, are co-existing rather than inter-mingling. In the first place this fusion of modernity and tradition must be achieved so that tourist life does not appear something incongruous, stuck on to a background completely foreign to it. But even more, the exact future of this industry must be calculated as precisely as possible, for it only needs some international crisis or some alteration in the rate of exchange, and all these luxury hotels could be empty; the islanders will then have to cut their losses and rediscover where their true wealth lies. The risk they run is predominantly an economic one. Until what we may call this tourist revolution, life in the islands was sufficiently varied to avoid any possibility of the economy becoming unbalanced. If speculation in the tourist industry increases, might not the islands, simply because they are islands, become too easily affected by outside emergencies? In the same way as some islands depend on a single crop introduced from outside, be it spices, copra, cocoa or sugar-canes, is it not playing for rather high stakes to turn the Balearic Islands into exclusively tourist islands?

It is only the islanders who run this risk, and we have to realize that there are still plenty of sites to develop. In fact the tourist industry is precarious only to a very relative extent. The tide unleased a few years ago cannot be reversed. The number of foreigners increased by 25.3 per cent between 1963 and 1964; and a new hotel is opened very two days four hours forty-eight minutes. If some crisis were to shake the tourist industry to its foundations, it would not be confined to Spain, and still less to the Balearic Islands. Since holidaymakers come to the islands from all over Europe, all Europe would have to be threatened with ruin. Little by little a civilization is taking shape in which leisure hours are important, and all far-seeing governments are developing such sites as they now have at their disposal, in order to deal with this tourist boom. In the Balearic Islands, the only likely change is a qualitative one. At one time they attracted wealthy travellers with many weeks to spare; they stayed until they thought they had seen and experienced everything, and then went home. In the middle of the twentieth century, as we have seen, the flow of tourists became heavier and more popular; the bulk of 'customers' came from the great European cities. As the standard and the cost of living rise, we may wonder whether, when the development programmes of the Costa del Sol and the Languedoc coast in France are completed, the Balearic Islands may not arrive in less than ten years at the point which it took Saint Tropez and Capri half a century to reach; that is, become the monopoly of a certain class of well-to-do people.

Whatever its nature may be, the future of the tourist industry is assured, since it fulfils one of man's basic needs. For about twenty years the same phenomenon has appeared at every holiday season: a general exodus from the cities and their daily routine. Increasingly, this deep longing has led us southwards, to the shores of the Mediterranean where we can be almost sure of the sun throughout the summer.

But why is it that some travellers stay on the mainland beaches, while others storm the horizon by plane or boat, in quest of islands? It is more than a taste for the exotic, or love of the sun, or the friendly welcome of the islanders; what fascinates certain people is the feeling of being beyond the whole world, a tiny speck in a great infinity. Lawrence Durrell, in *Reflections on a Marine Venus*, suggests an amusing explanation of these 'islomanes'; they are the direct descendants of the Atlanteans, 'and it is towards the lost Atlantic that their subconscious yearns throughout their island life'.

And there are perhaps other reasons, too, why some of us become 'islomanes' in spite of ourselves. There is the need to get away from ourselves, and at the same time the delight of seeing ourselves in our true proportions, as we must when we lie on a soft sandy beach and know that beyond the headlands, beyond the mountains, there is still the sea. And perhaps the secret of the Balearic Islands lies in the fact that among the great creations of nature they have the rare gift of remaining within the grasp of man's understanding.

Bibliography

of works not mentioned in the text

AUBERT DE LA RUE, *L'homme et les îles*, Paris 1947.

BALAGUER Y BOSCH, *Compendio de geografia e historia de les Baleares*. Palma 1870.

BOLETIN DE LA SOCIEDAD ARQUEOLOGICA LULIANA. Palma.

BOURDEAUX, *Guide du yachtman en Méditerranée*. Paris 1958.

BRASILLACH Robert, *Comme le temps passe*. Paris 1937.

BROUÉ P. et TÉMINE E., *La révolution et la guerre d'Espagne*. Paris 1961.

CABANELLAS J., *Le cicerone français à Palma de Majorque*. Palma 1845.

COMPANER Y FUENTÈS A., *Dominacion islamita en las Baleares*. Palma 1888.

COSTA, *Las cuevas de Mallorca*. Palma 1945.

COSTA, *Guide de Majorque*. Palma 1960.

COMPTE-POSTA R., *Conoce Vd a Mallorca?* Palma 1951.

DAVILLIER CH et DORÉ G., *Voyage à Majorque*. Paris 1862.

DEFFONTAINES et DURLIAT, *Catalogne*. Paris 1957.

DEFFONTAINES et DURLIAT, *Levant*. Paris 1957.

DEFFONTAINES et DURLIAT, *Baléares*, Paris 1957.

DEFFONTAINES P., *Etude de l'habitation aux Baléares* (Sociedad de Historia Natural). Palma 1956.

DERVENN Cl., *Les Baléares*. Paris 1935.

DOLFUSS L., *Etudes sur le Moyen Age espagnol*. Paris 1884.

DURLIAT M., *Histoire du Roussillon*. Paris 1962.

ENSENYAT B., *Chant à Majorque*. Palma 1953.

ESCALAS, *Guide de Majorque*. Palma 1964.

ESTADA E., *La Ciudad de Palma*. Palma 1892.

FAYOL A., *Baléares, îles heureuses*. Paris 1932.

FERRA BARTOMEU, *Chopin et George Sand à Majorque*. Palma 1960.

FOURGOUS-LAVAL, *Les îles Baléares*. Paris 1957.

GAUBERT E., *La Majorquine*. Paris 1917.

GUIDE BLEU, *Baléares*. Paris 1957.

LAMEIRE Irénée, *Les occupations militaires de l'île de Majorque*. Paris 1908.

LLINARÈS A., *Ramon Llull, philosophe de l'action*. Paris 1964.

LLADO Y FARRAGUT, *Carlos I y Alcudia durante la Germania*. Palma 1959.

LLOPIS A., *Ibiza*. Barcelona 1956.

MACABICH-LLOBET, *Historia de Ibiza, Corsarios ibicencos*. Ibiza 1917.

MACKENZIE-MOLLY, *Stories of Majorca*. Palma 1961.

MACKENZIE-MOLLY, *The Royal House of Majorca*. Palma 1962.

MARTEL E. A., *Les cavernes de Majorque*. Paris 1903.

MERRIEN J., *Petits ports d'à côté*. Paris 1962.

MONOD J., *Majorque*. Palma 1945.

MONOGRAFIAS MENORQUINAS, Ciudadela 1950.

MORAND P. et ARIELLI, *Majorque*. Barcelona 1962.

PANORAMA BALEAR, (petites monographies; plus de 50 volumes). Palma.

PIFFERER P., *Islas Baleares*. Barcelona 1888.

PILLEMENT G., *Les cathédrales d'Espagne*. Paris 1952.

RETZ [DE] (cardinal), *Mémoires*.

RIPOLL Luis, *La catedral de Mallorca*. Palma 1945.

SANTANER-MARI Juan, *Geografia de las Baleares*. Palma 1958.

SCHULEKAMP, *Les îles Baléares*. Paris 1964.

SOLBERG Th., *Some notes on the Balearic Islands*. Chicago 1929.

SPRINGORUM, *Majorque*. Berne 1959.

SYDOW B. E., COLFS-CHANAYE D. et CHANAYE S., *Lettres de Chopin et de G. Sand (1836-1839)*. Palma 1960.

VASSAL Dr, 'Le mouvement touristique des îles Baléares'. *Terre-Air-Mer*, juillet-août 1933, Paris.

VUILLIER G., *Les îles oubliées: Les Baléares, la Corse, la Sardaigne*. Paris 1893.

VALDEFLEUR [DE] P. D., *Bernat, l'aveugle des Baléares*. Nancy 1960.

VERDAGUER M., *Un verano en Mallorca*. Barcelona 1959.

VICTORY-MANELLA J., *Menorca*. Mahon 1948.

VILLALONGA L., *Majorque*. Barcelona 1960.

Explanatory List of Illustrations

The following explanatory list relates to the illustrations to be found all together at the end of this book, except for the colour plates and maps which are placed as indicated below.

BLACK AND WHITE PLATES

1. ON THE PASEO MARITIMO AT PALMA.

2. PALMA. THE MILLS OF ES JONQUET.

3. THE PALMA YACHTING CLUB. Sailing, a particularly glamorous form of tourism, is becoming increasingly popular in the Balearic Islands. The deeply indented coastline of the islands provides sailors with an infinite variety of *calas*, creeks and harbours. The Palma Yachting Club, one of the most important in Spain, has more than 300 members with vessels of all sizes.

4. PALMA CATHEDRAL SEEN FROM THE FISHING PORT.

5 and 6. LA LONJA. James I, immediately after the conquest, decided to assist trade in the port of Palma by building a kind of Stock Exchange for the merchants. In 1293 he made over the land necessary for building, but it was not until the middle of the fifteenth century that work began. Apart from the cathedral, it is the building which best evokes the golden age of the maritime kingdom of the Balearic Islands. This masterpiece of Gothic civil architecture was designed by the Majorcan Guillermo Sagrera, the architect of the cathedral of Perpignan; it consists of a huge rectangular hall flanked by four octagonal towers and supported by six pillars which spread out like palm-trees.

7. THE CONSULATE OF THE SEA. This was built at the beginning of the seventeenth century, and was a tribunal where all cases involving maritime law were heard. The building, in the Renaissance style, today houses a museum embodying all the maritime traditions of Majorca.

8. THE ALMUDAINA. This is the name given to the group of buildings near the cathedral which was built by the Moors as the palace of the Walis. It was completely reconstructed at the time of the Conquest and became the king's palace. Then when the Majorcan court no longer existed, it was occupied by the representative of the king of Aragon. Nowadays the offices of the Captain-general and the *Tribunal de la Audiencia* are housed there, and its official status limits sightseeing.

9. PICTURESQUE HORSE-DRAWN VEHICLES ON THE PASEO SAGRERA.

10. PALMA CATHEDRAL. After the Conquest, James I built the 'Chapel of the Trinity' which was the first building on the site, and dates from the begin-

73

ning of the fourteenth century (about 1310). The great apse could not be built until embankments had been made on the side facing the sea. In 1327 this work was finished. The nave was built under the direction of the Majorcan architect Jaime Mates, from 1368 onwards. Different chapels were added later. At the beginning of the fifteenth century the cathedral consisted of half the building we see today; it was completed in the sixteenth century. The west door dates from 1592 and the great rose window in the façade from 1596. The cathedral was not consecrated until 1601, almost three centuries after work on it began. The result is a majestic, well-lit building; the central nave, with its high windows, is supported by massive buttresses which lend character to the exterior. The whole cathedral has often been likened to 'a great organ in masonry'. The image is enhanced by the warm golden glow of the Santañy limestone of which it is built. 'No Gothic building, except perhaps Santa Maria de la Mar at Barcelona, has ever provided so much usable space at so little cost. It is the finest victory of mind over matter the Middle Ages ever achieved' (Pierre Lavedan). The 'Seu', or 'Seo', as the Majorcans call it, contains the tombs of King James II and King James III. It must however be noted that the bold lines of the various master builders resulted in a building which collapsed on several occasions. The history of Palma Cathedral, 'as full of miscalculations as that of Beauvais, helps us to understand the limitations of mediaeval techniques' (Marcel Durliat).

11. PALMA CATHEDRAL. Over the Mirador doorway has been placed what was originally the high altar. This delicately carved work has been attributed to Antonio Camprodon, a sculptor from Perpignan whose life and work illustrate the close artistic and political interdependence of the Balearic Islands and the south of France.

12. THE BAY OF PALMA BY NIGHT. As soon as the wonderful Mediterranean night falls on the town, the chief monuments on the bay are floodlit.

13, 14, 15. BELLVER. The castle of Bellver, high above the Bay of Palma, is one of the most famous buildings in Majorca. According to Jovellanos, it is 'one of the best military edifices of the fourteenth century' (*Memorias historicas sobre el Castello de Bellver*, Palma 1813). Its ground-plan is a circle, which is unusual in Spain; it consists of a circular rampart and four towers. We may wonder whether this is not an adaptation of the plan used for Friedrich von Hohenstauffen at Castel del Monte in southern Italy. If this is so, Bellver would be a concrete expression of the close ties we know to have existed between the Balearic Islands and Italy under the kings of Majorca. The castle was built at the beginning of the fourteenth century in the Catalan style; it combines regard for military needs with remarkable aesthetic feeling. Innumerable historical events are connected with it. It was originally the summer residence of the island's rulers, but was soon turned into a prison. For the French it has particularly poignant associations, since it was there that some of the French prisoners held in the Balearic Islands after Dupont's defeat at Bailen (1808) were detained. The remnants of the army first suffered the ordeal of the prison-ships at Cadiz, and were then sent to the Balearic Islands. A large contingent was left on Ibiza, and

5,500 were sent to the quarantine camp at Port Mahon on Minorca. The others, about 10,000 of them, were left on Cabrera in May 1809, and kept in appalling conditions. Several cases of cannibalism were reported. There were fifteen women in these camps, deprived of food and water as they were. The higher-ranking officers, after a short detention at Palma, were imprisoned in the castle of Bellver, leaving on its walls several inscriptions which can still be seen today. Although the English agreed after the capitulation of Bailen that the French troops should be repatriated, it was not until 1814 that the survivors were freed and returned home.

16 and 17. THE CLOISTER OF SAN FRANCISCO, standing against the church which contains the tomb of the 'doctor illuminatus', Ramon Llull. It was begun in 1281, and King James I laid the first stone. Whereas the church, though contemporary with the cloister, is not homogeneous in style (following a fire, Francisco de Herrera rebuilt the great door in a seventeenth century baroque idiom) the cloister is a perfect example of Gothic architecture. Until the nineteenth century it was inhabited by Franciscan monks. As we stand beneath these columns we cannot but think of the task undertaken by one of the most illustrious members of the community, Fray Junipero Serra. This monk, born at Petra, a little white Majorcan village, at the beginning of the eighteenth century, went as a missionary to the New World, and discovered a country, California, whose name is Majorcan in origin. It is said, in fact, that when Brother Serra arrived in these remote parts, he exclaimed, 'Cal' de forn!' which is to say in Castilian 'Calor de horno', (hot as an oven). Brother Serra founded the towns of San Carlos, San Diego, San Luis, San Francisco, Los Angeles and Sacramento, and when he died in 1784 it was the end of an extraordinary life. His missionary travels are an illustration of the islander's gift for bringing with him something of his own small homeland, however distant and vast the lands he visits. He was one of the last *conquistadores* of the faith; born as he was in a humble peasant home, the visions we see, as it were superimposed in the delicate sculpture of the cloister of San Francisco, are of that great order of preaching friars, and, even more clearly, of his own evangelization of California.

18. STREET IN THE OLD QUARTER OF PALMA. At every turn we see a porch or a church tower between two rows of buildings in warm golden stone. Santa Cruz, Santa Eulalia, San Jaime, Santa Magdalena, Santa Margarita, San Miguel, are the churches which lift their towers above the cool streets where bells ring from earliest dawn. The bell-tower in the picture is that of Nuestra Señora del Socorro, one of the most characteristic examples of the baroque style of the Balearic Islands; there are many others both at Palma and in the towns of Alcudia, Inca and Binisalem, as well as on Minorca (the dome of San Francisco and Nuestra Señora del Rosario).

19. PALMA. CALLE DE LA SEO. This street going up to the old town follows the walls of the palace belonging to Juan March, one of the most extraordinary figures of the twentieth-century business world, whose life could serve as subject for a fantastic novel.

20. OLD STREET IN PALMA.

21. CALLE DE LA ALMUDAINA.   This arch, a relic of the Saracen period, was one of the five gateways of the ancient citadel of the Emirs.

22. COURTYARD OF THE CASA OLEZA.   The palaces or aristocratic residences of Palma, taken as a whole, are architecturally most interesting. They belonged for the most part to important bourgeois families who had amassed their fortunes on the sea or in Italy. At the beginning of the seventeenth century, many palaces were built in Palma on the sites of mediaeval houses dating from the time of the Conquest; they are in the delicate Renaissance style, and today they give this Mediterranean port a charm comparable to that of Rome. They have a large interior courtyard or patio, either square or rectangular, with a monumental staircase on one side, an arcade supported by slender columns, and often, in the courtyard, a well with graceful wrought-iron decoration. Generally there are two floors, the rooms of which are richly adorned with fine furniture and tapestries. Among the best-known houses in Palma, apart from the Oleza, are the Casa Conde de Peralada, the Casa Vivat, and Casas Oleo, Palma, Berga, Puigdorfila, and Marquès de Solleric. They were the principal residence of rich families, but they were not occupied all the year round. In spring or autumn the whole household set out for villas about five to seven miles from the capital; these too were really palatial, but their chief adornment was a garden which brought consummate art to bear in the use of natural beauty. A whole mode of life is expressed in this architecture, these courtyards, and these gardens.

23 and 24.   PALMA.   SAN FRANCISCO.

25 and 26.   THE GARDENS OF MAJORCA: ALFABIA AND RAIXA.   The estate of Alfabia, dating from the fourteenth century, might almost have come straight out of the Arabian Nights. The garden, the tropical plants, the fountains, the flights of doves, all bring to mind an eastern Paradise. At Raixa, the same splendour is there, but with more of an Italian, humanist tinge. It seems still to be haunted by the memory of the great Cardinal Despuig, an illustrious figure and a famous collector and archaeologist of the eighteenth century.

27.   PALMA.   PATIO OF THE CASA CONDE DE PERALADA.

28.   MIRAMAR.   In the steps of Ramon Llull. . . .

29.   RAIXA.

30 and 31.   VALLDEMOSA.   Perched on the hillside at a height of 1,300 feet this village is one of the most beautiful and also the most famous in the Balearic Islands. Immediately after the Conquest, the Majorcan kings were attracted by the natural beauty of the place and built there a palace comparable with the one which still exists today at Sineu. Unfortunately the palace at Valldemosa was completely destroyed. At present the chief interest of the place lies in the houses which enshrine the memory of Santa Catalina Tomas, and in the vast Carthusian monastery of the seventeenth and eighteenth centuries. In the nineteenth century the monks were forced to leave by the upheavals of 1835, and two famous people stayed there— George Sand and Chopin. They arrived by the steamship El *Mallorquin* on

November 8, 1839, and began by spending six days in a boarding-house in Palma itself. They lived for more than a month at Establiments, in the suburbs, but were turned out by their landlord. On December 13th the travellers took up residence in three of the monastery cells. Chopin was able to continue working, but had to wait for his piano, a Pleyel, which was kept by the Customs for a very long time. It finally arrived on January 13th. 'Chopin composed most of his preludes there, and made the final version of those he had merely sketched beforehand. He also wrote the second Ballade in F major, opus 38, the two Polonaises, in A major and in C minor, opus 40, and the Mazurka in E minor, opus 41 no. 2. The Sonata in B flat minor and the two Nocturnes opus 37 were probably composed in Majorca.' (B. Ferra, *Chopin et George Sand à Majorque*). But on February 11th, for reasons that are now well-known, they returned to Palma and thence to Barcelona. This ninety-seven-day episode in the island formed the subject of a book called *Un hiver à Majorque*, which George Sand published on returning to France.

32 and 33. AT VALLDEMOSA. Chopin's piano, now lonely and silent. Every day a pious hand lays on the yellowed ivory of the keyboard a rose picked on the terrace, in the little garden. To Chopin, the cloister was 'full of ghostly terrors' as George Sand wrote. The whitewashed walls, and the long corridors swept by the January wind, form a setting forever haunted by the shades of this romantic couple.

34. PALMA: EL BORNE, PALMA'S PRINCIPAL AVENUE. At the usual time for *tapas*, that is to say about 1.30 p.m. and 7 p.m., the crowd comes here to stroll around. The avenue is bordered by luxury shops, tourist agencies and pavement cafés. It is beneath these leafy branches that the true heart of the capital beats.

35. ANDRAITX: THE CASTLE. Inner courtyard.

36. THE ISLAND OF DRAGONERA seen from the *trappa*.

37. THE PORT AND VILLAGE OF ANDRAITX, about three miles apart, have become one of the most attractive and most recent tourist centres in the island. The port itself has contrived to carry on a relatively active fishing industry. It is used as a harbour by boats coming mainly from Tarragona and the Catalan ports, and also from Valencia; but an increasing number of yachts also put in there.

38. THE DECORATED STERN OF AN OLD COASTER.

39. THE BELVEDERE OF RICARDO ROCA.

40. THE BELVEDERE OF LAS ANIMAS.
These two watch-towers, or *atalayas*, are situated near the villages of Estellenchs and Bañalbufar.

41. NEAR THE COLL DE SA GREMOLA on the Andraitx-Estellenchs road.

42. NEAR ESTELLENCHS: flock of sheep grazing under the olive-trees.

43. LA FORADADA, or pierced rock, is one of the headlands which contribute to the splendour of Son Marroig, chosen by the Archduke Louis Salvador of Austria for the site of his house.

44. THE PUERTO DE SOLLER. The bay, which is almost completely landlocked, is becoming increasingly popular with tourists and pleasure-seekers.

45. THE SOLLER AMPHITHEATRE. The village and port of Soller which are beautifully situated in a mountain landscape, are an important tourist centre. Apart from the textile industry, this region makes its living from citrus fruits, particularly oranges, which grow on the slopes by the village of Fornalutx.

46. THE ROOFS OF THE MONASTERY OF LLUCH. Lluch crouches in a valley at a height of 1,300 feet, and its monastery was built in the seventeenth century. It is the centre of the traditional pilgrimage to the Moreneta, the statue of the Virgin who is the patroness of the Majorcans. But the greatest charm of Lluch lies in its approaches; for example the Pollensa road which climbs up between eroded limestone cliffs through the Vall d'en March which is as startling to look at as any Far Western landscape. In the immediate neighbourhood of Lluch, La Calobra, the Torrente de Pareis, and the Gorch-Blau are spots especially worth seeing.

47 and 48. OLIVE-TREES. Visitors find a continual source of amazement in the olive groves, with their bark the colour of an elephant's hide. The branches with their fantastic serpentine curves, the trunks twisted like giant figures of Atlas, seem to take on every imaginable shape. Some creep like boa constrictors, others appear to be in the throes of a convulsion. Huge masses are held to the ground by slender threads; others, swollen and curved like the hindquarters of some strange beast, seem to stretch out clawed feet. The effect is one of delirium, of constantly shifting patterns. Surely there are witches in a wood like this! And the olive branch, that symbol of peace, seems oddly remote and out of place here.

49 to 52. BAIX DE PUIG. Gathering almonds in the month of August.

53. CA'N PILO. Feeding-time for the goats.

54. DOVES AT MIRAMAR.

55. NEAR LA PUEBLA: woman drawing water at a noria.
However hard the peasants work, these scenes of country life are often accompanied by singing; and the threshing floors often re-echo to the sound of chants known as *tonadas del batre*. The unspoilt simplicity of country life in the Balearic Islands was for a long time a fruitful source of strange superstitions. In Majorca, for instance, there was *mal boci* or sore mouth, transmitted by one individual to another by the swallowing of some morsel upon which, naturally, a wizard had cast a spell. Magicians, called *curanderos*, *bruixes* or *bruxots*, cast spells on various objects at the request of their customers, who, without hesitation, paid generously for such 'services'. In this island with its peasant population, the sea has had little influence on the language and thought of the inland people; very few proverbs or dialect expressions refer to it. Though so much of Majorcan folklore and community life has its roots in the land, the land does not belong to those who till it, except in the tiny fragmented plots around Palma or the Bay of Alcudia (Muro, La Puebla). In the almond-growing plains and on Minorca, land is held in more or less the same way as in certain regions of the Spanish

mainland: a few important families possess vast estates which are let to tenant farmers.

56. TERRACED FIELDS NEAR BANALBUFAR. The villages of Estellenchs and Bañalbufar, built on the hillside, are especially picturesque. The steep slopes are covered with wild flowers, and stone walls have been built to hold up the earth of the small gardens in which the principal crop is tomatoes. Life in this part of island has changed considerably since the coast road from Andraitx to Estellenchs was built.

57. FLOCK OF SHEEP NEAR SON VERI.

58. PEASANTS AT LA PUEBLA (note the rustic type of fork).

59. THRESHING GRAIN NEAR LA PUEBLA.

60. STEPS UP TO THE CALVARIO AT POLLENSA. On the right are the Vicens workshops, one of the most important centres of Majorcan craftsmanship.

61. THE CHURCH AT SELVA, dating from the fourteenth century. It still possesses an interesting bay with an ogival vault.

62. POLLENSA: the procession known as *Es devellment* which takes place on the slopes leading to the Calvario, on the evening of Good Friday.

63. THE CALM WATERS OF THE BAY OF POLLENSA.

64. THE ROCK OF ES COLOMER on the road to Formentor.

65. THE BELVEDERE OF ES COLOMER.

66. BEACH SUNSHADES AT FORMENTOR.

67, 68 and 69. 'TARDE DE TOROS' AT ALCUDIA. A village corrida is quite an occasion. First come the advance notices; the walls of the houses are covered with multicoloured posters with the names of the three *novilleros* splashed all over them in large letters. Then, on the Friday, the six bulls arrive and are put into an enclosure. The urchins and the young men are aware of this, and as night falls they prowl 'by chance' around the corral in the old bastion in the ramparts. On the Saturday the experts enjoy their sacred right – to run their hands over the animals. These experts are the toreros and their assistants. Their three names are written on three pieces of paper, and lots are drawn; each one knows which bulls he is to fight. In the little square, at about ten in the evening, the cafés come to life. People are watching television, but the subject of conversation begins to narrow down, particularly in the *Circulo Alcudiense*. Everyone it talking about tomorrow's event. About noon on the Sunday, after Mass, the Plaza de General Franco is crowded. At about two o'clock the place is deserted; everyone has gone to lunch. At about three, the cafés are full again, the women and children dressed in their Sunday best. Three yellow taxis make their way through the crowd and reach the *Circulo*. The toreros are arriving 'in mufti'. Swiftly they climb the three flights of stairs to the top of the house. Trunks and suitcases follow them – their costumes, cloaks and swords. Assistants pass them shirt or trousers, making sure that nothing is forgotten. There is no panic, only clear, precise orders, but the atmosphere is tense. Almost simultaneously they each withdraw into silence before the *Virgen*. A few moments pass. Outside, the square is swarming with people, and the noise reaches

79

the toreros despite the high building. The *Banda municipal*, all their brass gleaming, breaks into sound, as though serenading the toreros. Then the noise moves into the distance, taking with it the crowd to the sound of a march. Quietly, the toreros come down, and drive to the arena. The day brightens. The festival is about to begin. The stone seats, hot with the sun, are filling up. Beyond the highest of the rose-pink stones is the bay of Pollensa and the sierras of Formentor. The president of the corrida arrives, escorted by a platoon of green-uniformed guards. A bell rings, there is the salute of the *cuadrilla*, and the door of the *toril* opens. Every Sunday, in almost every village in the Balearic Islands, the same scene is repeated. But the crowds are densest in Palma (where the arena is the sixth largest in Spain). Few great matadors are Majorcans. The centre where bull-fighting is the greatest draw is the little village of Muro, in the interior. Bulls are not bred in the island; they come from the mainland, by air, the Thursday or Friday before they are due to be killed.

70. ALCUDIA. PUERTA DE MUELLE. In the north-east of the island, thirty-three miles from Palma, is Alcudia, one of the most interesting villages in Majorca. It stands on the bay which faces east, that is to say towards Rome, Greece and Phoenicia; it has lived through all the invasions, and the last, that of the Moors, gave it its name, Al Kudia, the hill. Only two gates remain of the fortifications that protected it. All that remains of a second wall, the rampart of San Fernando, built under Philip III, is one bastion, which has now been turned into an arena, on the Bay of Pollensa. In the sixteenth and seventeenth centuries, the town passed through a period of relative prosperity, reflected in the houses bordering the narrow main street, with their carved windows in Renaissance style, and arched main doorways. Alcudia is essentially a country town, but nowadays it is becoming an intellectual centre. The painter Miro stays there for long periods. The Bryan archaeological foundation is engaged in listing local places of interest, such as the excavations of Ca'n Picafort, the Roman theatre on the road to the Puerto, and the town of *Pollentia* near the church. The restoration of the ramparts, begun during the winter of 1964-1965, will bring back the original appearance of the walled town which has been called the 'Avila of Majorca'.

71 and 72. THE TOMBS OF CA'N PICAFORT. The excavations at Son Real, about a mile and a quarter from Ca'n Picafort, have led to the discovery of two main sites: a burial ground on the shore and an islet containing tombs, separated by a distance of about 500 yards. On the islet of Los Porros three large tombs have been found, hollowed out of the earth and looking like rooms supported by a central pillar. Up to the present, two of these have been excavated. On the shore itself at Son Real there are seventy-two tombs in all, which can be divided into three different types: rectangular, round (of which there are five) and apsidal. The best preserved are the rectangular ones, which can be seen in the photograph. There are seven of these altogether. Besides the tombs, about 2,000 skeletons have been found, together with a few ornaments which show that these people used bronze and iron; but no inscription has been discovered to give an exact indication of their origin. It is generally thought that this was a nucleus of population

which came from the eastern Mediterranean between the fifth and third centuries B.C. Since only a burial ground has been uncovered, we are now faced with the question of where the town was. It is probably still buried beneath the dense cloak of pine forests along the shore. The site of Ca'n Picafort is an extremely interesting one. The work of excavation is being done by American and Spanish archaeologists under the aegis of the Bryan Foundation of Alcudia. There may still lie buried there an important series of documents which will increase our knowledge of the ancient history of the Balearic Islands and the Mediterranean.

73. THE ROMAN THEATRE AT ALCUDIA (on the road between the village and the port), which was recently uncovered through the work of the Bryan Foundation. Not long ago the view from these stepped seats, burning hot from the sun, was one of the most beautiful in the island. This panorama is considerably altered today by the building of new tourist hotels. Surely one of the most beautiful spots in the island could have been better protected?

74. ROMAN BRIDGE AT POLLENSA, on the road leading to Lluch. This is one of the relics of the Roman occupation of the Balearic Islands. The most easily visible traces of the conquest are in the eastern part of Majorca, on the bays of Pollensa and Alcudia, and on Minorca, in the town of Ciudadela. The colony of *Pollentia* was on the site where Alcudia now stands. The remains of the ancient capital founded by Quintus Caecilius Metellus consist of a Roman theatre (on the road to Puerto Alcudia) and the foundations of houses near the church at Alcudia, which have been excavated by the Bryan Foundation. The Roman town of Pollentia is of extreme interest to archaeologists, and slightly resembles that of Ampurias on the Catalan coast. The excavations show at least six different levels dating from the founding of the city up to its destruction in the fourth century A.D. Statues, ornaments and coins can be seen in the Archaeological Museum in Puerto d'Alcudia.

75. ARTA. The church and oratory of San Salvador on the summit of the hill.

76. THE WALLS OF CAPDEPERA. This town, founded by King Sancho, is dominated by a rampart dating from the beginning of the fourteenth century; it is a good example of the fortification of a new town, very similar to those in Languedoc. The chapel, built on the highest point, dates from 1323. The present town, which is much more recent, is below the walls, which now protect only ruins.

77. ARTA. The tower of Cañamel is one of the remains of the fortifications built on the island after the conquest. Each piece of land granted by the king to the colonists was protected against pirate raids by constructions of this type, of which a few other examples survive, notably at Manacor.

78 to 81. MAJORCAN NATIVE DRESS AND MUSICAL INSTRUMENTS. The present way of life on the islands and their attraction for tourists have made it possible to resurrect folk-groups like those of Valldemosa, Puente d'Inca or Selva. Sometimes a few solo performers cycle round the island giving concerts on the beach or outside cafés crowded with tourists. The traditional Majorcan male costume is rather like that of the Bretons, with baggy

trousers, a waistcoat and a round hat. The most frequently used musical instruments apart from fiddle and guitar are the *tamboril*, a sort of drum, the *chirima*, a sort of bombardon, and the *gaeta* or pipe. Boys and girls dance to rhythms some of which are directly inherited from the Arabs. The chief dances today are the *bolero*, *jotas* and *mateixas*, and *copeos*. As for the songs, there are of course love-songs, but there are also songs relating to the various types of farm-work done throughout the year: fig-picking (*figuerail*), sheep-shearing (*tosa*), and above all pig-killing (*ses matances*). Naturally enough, the words are in the local dialect, which is so near to certain Languedoc patois that southern French and Majorcans can sometimes understand each other without great difficulty if they meet in the course of a holiday. But we must realize that although *Mallorquin* and *Ibicenco* are still generally spoken, the songs and dances survive only through the efforts of scholars like B. Ensenuyat, or through the work of the folk-groups which are such a delight to tourists in search of local colour.

82 and 83. THE CAVES OF CAMPANET. These caves, situated near the twin villages of Buger and Campanet on the road from Palma to Alcudia, were discovered and opened to the public in about 1950. They complete Majorca's marvellous series of caves, the others being at Arta, Porto Cristo (caves of the Dragon and caves of Hams) and Genova. Here we have not only the beautiful underground formations, but also the perfect neatness of the terraced gardens, and the view from the oratory of San Miguel.

84. VIEW OF PORTO CRISTO from the garden of the Cuevas del Drach.

85. THE BEACH AT SAN TELMO (near Andraitx). In this bay lies the islet of Pantalleu where King James the Conqueror is said to have landed. Nowadays a large number of hotels have been built along the creeks where undersea fishing enthusiasts can visit the most beautiful underwater scenery in the island.

86. PUERTO D'ALCUDIA: main wing of the building known as Ciudad Blanca. This example of modern architecture gives a good idea of the type of building to which the tourist industry is giving rise. Each flat is self-contained, thanks to the ingenious way in which the façade is divided.

87. CALA FIGUERA.

88. PORTO PETRO.
These are two good examples of harbours where people taking a sailing holiday can put in.

89. YOUNG EMBROIDERESSES AT PALMA.

90. MINORCA. The port of Mahon. The deep fjord, almost eight miles long, and the sheltered stretches of water decided the future of Port Mahon; it had to be a port and naval base. Sixty years of English occupation, and then six years with the French in the island, left traces which can still be seen today. Besides the town itself, there is what was formerly George Town, now called Villa Carlos (in the background on the right) which possesses some remarkable barrack buildings. On the islet in the middle of the inlet was the quarantine camp which housed some of the prisoners of Bailen, and, in 1830, soldiers wounded in the Algerian campaign. Part of the town has

an atmosphere full of touches quite foreign to the 'Spanishness' of the island, such as the classical façade of the archive building, the bow windows of the houses, the rocking-chairs to be glimpsed within, and the liberal curiosity of the Ateneo, which goes back to the days of Orfila who was one of the greatest doctors in nineteenth-century Paris.

91. THE PORT OF MAHON.

92. THE PORT OF MAHON. A regatta on the calm expanse of water. On the top of the hill is a house in the English colonial style (eighteenth century) which is said to have been visited by Lady Hamilton.

93. THE PORT OF MAHON IN 1841. View from San Antonio. A squadron of the French fleet is putting into harbour.

94. CALA DE SANTA GOLDANA (five miles from Ferrieras).

95. THE TOWN OF VILLA CARLOS (formerly George Town) founded by the English in the eighteenth century. Its vast esplanade is bordered with barracks.

96. SAN LUIS: the morning of August 25th. All the streets are decorated for the patronal festival; there is to be a procession in the afternoon, and in the evening the whole village will celebrate. In the Balearic Islands, these patronal festivals are an intensely important part of both town and country life; their interest is one of folklore as well as religion. The strangest festival in Minorca is that of Saint John, which takes place in Ciudadela on June 23rd.

97. THE LITTLE VILLAGE OF SAN LUIS, near Port Mahon. When this picture was taken, there had been a death in one of these white houses, and only a few hours afterwards, the funeral was taking place at the church. In almost the same way as in Moslem countries, the dead are buried after only twenty-four hours. Where the towns of Majorca give a light golden-brown effect, Minorca appears white. In the summer sunlight, a little village like San Luis is dazzling. Everything here is white-washed. The village itself is one of the most perfect survivals of the French occupation in the eighteenth century. It was a completely new creation, planned from scratch on Crown land ('*appartenant au Roy*', as the French documents have it), and laid out on rectangular lines. The church, neo-classical in style, bears an inscription on a band across the façade: *Divo Ludovico Sacrum Dedicavere Galli An MDCCLXI*, and a medallion with the arms of Louis XV, whose representative was the governor Yacinthe-Cajetan, Comte de Lannion. This façade, apart from its architectural interest, is in a way an affirmation of the Catholic faith. The English had, in fact, during their occupation, transformed the church of San Francisco at Ciudadela into a Protestant place of worship. As soon as the French arrived, they quickly re-established the traditional cult. In addition, the French occupation brought with it the régime which followed the revocation of the Edict of Nantes. When the Comte de Lannion and his aide Caussan decided to build San Luis, the village and its church took on a significance at once political, economic and religious. French influence is especially alive here, but for a long time the whole of Minorca remembered and handed down the tales of these successive waves of occupa-

83

tion that broke over the island, changing its official religion, coinage, system of taxation, language, way of life and political opinions.

98. FORNELLS. A little fishing port on the northern coast of the island.

99. 'TAULA' AND 'TALAYOT' AT TREPUCO. The Balearic Islands possess a very large number of megalithic monuments which can be divided into several types. On Majorca there are more than a thousand *talayots*. They are ruins, round or square in shape, made up of enormous blocks of stone held in place by their own weight; no trace of mortar or cement has been found. They probably served as watchtowers in the ramparts surrounding villages, and are outwardly similar to the nuraghi of Sardinia. Generally all dwellings have been destroyed and only these fortifications remain. The *talayots* have given their name to a civilization which began to flourish about 1200 B.C. These buildings are seen in both Majorca and Minorca. In the latter island, archaeologists have discovered two other types of ruin: first the *taula*, a sort of stone table standing on a vertical pillar (the whole effect is T-shaped) which seems to have had some religious function. Then the *naveta*, so named because of its similarity to the hull of an upturned boat. The *naveta* at Es Tudons, roughly pyramidal in shape, is over thirty feet long. The interior consists of one room which contained various funerary objects, and would have served as burial-chamber for about fifty people. *Navetas*, *taulas* and *talayots* appear to be more or less contemporary. Minorca, however, offers a greater variety of examples.

100. MINORCAN COWS ON THE WAY TO MERCADAL.

101. 'NAVETA' AT ES TUDONS (near Ciudadela).

102. THE PORT OF CIUDADELA. This port lies in a *cala* about a kilometre long, in rather the same way as Port Mahon. The mail-boat from Alcudia leaves every Saturday about midday, loaded not only with passengers but also with cows, bulls and sheep. Minorca is still influenced by its larger neighbour as far as its history, language and exchange of ideas are concerned. The Minorcans, it is true, read the two newspapers published in the islands, *Baleares* and *Diario de Mallorca*, which are in Castilian. But ties almost as close unite them with Barcelona and Catalonia, for the same reason as with Majorca.

103. THE OBELISK IN THE SQUARE OF EL BORNE.

104. THE CHURCH OF THE ROSARY AT CIUDADELA: Churrigueresque doorway. This domed church, begun by the Dominicans in the seventeenth century, gives a fairly good idea of the splendour of baroque art in the Balearic Islands.

105. CIUDADELA. The arcaded houses, *Ses Voltes*, date from the eighteenth century. Ciudadela, at the end of the road built by Lord Kane, is the second city of the island. It was ousted from its position as capital when the English came in 1712, but still has a well-justified pride in its past glory. It is a town of arcaded streets and domed churches which are a relic of the Turkish occupation in 1558 (commemorated by an obelisk in the square of El Borne); it is also the seat of the bishopric. Here we are in another world. Despite the shoe factories in the outlying parts, the town belongs to another

age. Minorca is still the most unspoilt and best preserved of the Balearic Islands. It has been little affected by the tourist industry and remains comparatively isolated, living its own life – a life which, both in town and country, is independent and all its own.

106. A STREET IN CIUDADELA. A *guardia civil* is passing. The whole town seems drowsy; it is siesta time.

107. IBIZA FROM THE SEA. The town is dominated by its massive cathedral, which rises above one of the most complex fortification systems in the Mediterranean. The houses are like white cubes tumbled around the hillsides in studied confusion; they resemble the houses of the Maghrib, of the islands in the Aegean, and of the Lipari Islands, at one and the same time. Ibiza, then, is a port, but also a mighty fortress; the hill has been fortified since 1585, three years before the disaster of the Invincible Armada. The main gate (that of Las Tablas), as imposing as an Egyptian mastaba, bears the following inscription: *Philip II, unconquered king of Spain and the East Indies* (See no. 112).

108, 109 and 110. IBIZA: VIEW OF THE TOWN from the windows of the Ibiza museum, showing (no. 108) the bastion of Santa Lucia and one of the best-known archaeological sites in the island, the Illa Plana (which can be seen in no. 110). A large quantity of Carthaginian terra cotta statuettes was found there. On the other side of the town, on the site of Puig des Molins, a very large number of tombs (four or five thousand) has yielded a huge collection of objects including relatively more recent statues some of which are in the Ibiza museum. The museum has an immense collection including the famous head of a goddess (perhaps Tanit) in Hellenistic style.

111. IBIZA CATHEDRAL.

112. IBIZA. GATE OF LAS TABLAS.

113. THE FORTIFIED CHURCH OF SAN JORGE.

114. IBIZA. CALLE DE LA VIRGEN.

115. IBIZA. LA DRASSANETA. For years, fountains of this type have provided the entire water supply for a whole district of the 'capital', the permanent home of 15,000 people.

116. IBIZA MUSEUM: GREEK HEAD.

117. IBIZA MUSEUM. CATALAN ROMANESQUE HEAD OF CHRIST (twelfth century).

118. STREET IN SANTA EULALIA. The interior of the island is less impressive and less varied than that of Majorca, but less bare than that of Minorca. It contains a small number of villages that are perfect jewels, all white like the capital. Through Santa Eulalia flows the only watercourse in the island, and, in fact, in the whole archipelago! It is perhaps in these villages that the typical way of life of Ibiza has been most perfectly preserved. From the architectural point of view, the typical house of the island (like that of Formentera) is almost cubical in shape, with a flat terraced roof and no interior courtyard. There are very few openings in the walls, because of the strong sunlight. These cubes are built side by side as the size of the family increases; it is a kind of 'unit-plan architecture'. Salvador Dali did

exactly the same thing in his house at Port Lligat near Cadaqués, on the mainland.

119 and 120. WOMEN GOING TO CHURCH AT SAN JOSÉ. Although Ibiza cathedral was begun in the thirteenth century, it was not until the seventeenth that it reached the state in which we know it today. In the interior of the island the building of the village churches with their geometrical lines and whitewashed walls began as early as the fourteenth century; one of the most original of them is to be seen at San José. A portico with three arches stands in front of the main body of the building which is surmounted by an arcaded bell-tower. Other churches, such as that of San Jorge, are battlemented, bearing witness to the ultimate function of these buildings, which was not only religious, but also defensive. The costume of the women of Ibiza, which has been preserved intact up to the present day, consists mainly of a black skirt, long and full, falling in pleats over a wide petticoat, and sometimes brightened by a coloured apron. Over the shoulders is a small fringed shawl, very finely embroidered and often adorned with stylized flowers and geometrical designs. A small kerchief is worn on the head, its points tied beneath the chin, covering the plait, the end of which, tied with a large bow of coloured ribbon, hangs a few inches below it. This plait is sometimes very long in older women, and is one of the permanent elements of the traditional dress of Ibiza; the women wear it even with their working clothes in the fields. They wear *alpargatas* (rope-soled shoes) of a characteristic shape, half mules, half sandals, held on by a thin plaited cord round the ankle. As for the men's costumes, they no longer exist as a part of everyday life. They differed from those of the Majorcans, consisting of close-fitting white trousers, a long red sash (the *faja*), a white shirt with starched front, a black waistcoat, and the red *barratina*, a sort of cap turned down on one side, similar to those worn in Catalonia or Roussillon.

121. THE TOWN OF IBIZA. Since the tourist industry made its appearance, in comparative recent times, Ibiza has become a very important centre. Its exotic qualities and the beauty of the light in which it is bathed attract to the town itself visitors of a definite type—painters, students and writers.

122. CALA PORTINATX.

123. SAN ANTONIO ABAD. Another well-equipped tourist centre, frequented mainly by holiday-makers who enjoy surf-riding, undersea fishing, or simply doing nothing. Taking the Balearic Islands as a whole, Ibiza and Formentera are quite sharply divided from Majorca and Minorca. Whereas the two last are subject to the influence of Barcelona and Catalonia in general, the *Pithyuses* have close ties not only with Palma, but also with Alicante, Valencia and southern Spain.

124. ROOF OF THE CHURCH OF SANTA EULALIA.

125. CHURCH OF SAN MIGUEL.

126. CHURCH OF SANTA EULALIA.

127. WOMAN CARRYING WATER ON A ROAD IN IBIZA.

128. YOUNG GIRL AT EL PILAR (Formentera).

129. VIEW OF THE LOWER PART OF FORMENTERA. The island consists of a sort of tongue of flat land surrounded by salt-pans which were for a long time its entire wealth, rather than the wheat (*frumentum*) which gave it its name. Then at the other end there is a plateau of higher ground on which stands the village of El Pilar, a sort of Land's End. Out of the whole archipelago, this island suffered the raids of Moorish pirates for the greatest length of time. Its churches do not date from any earlier than the eighteenth century.

130. MILL ON FORMENTERA.

131. EL PILAR CHURCH (Formentera).

132. THE 'MOLA' ON FORMENTERA. The cliffs, 636 feet high, bear one of the thirty-seven lighthouses which mark the main headlands of the Balearic Islands. It is a last glimpse common to all who stand on the deck of a boat leaving the islands, feeling in their hearts a longing to return and experience again the happiest moments of their lives.

133. The Compagnie de Navigation Mixte, which serves the Balearic Islands, has laid on the stocks a new fast steamer of the car-ferry type, with a length of 420 feet and a tonnage of 6,000, capable of carrying 1,000 passengers. This floating garage will have the most modern equipment, air conditioning, stabilizers, a lido, sundeck and swimming bath, and closed-circuit television; it will carry 120 cars, embarked by means of five doors spaced along the sides and at the stern, without any hold-ups in the process. It will come into service at the beginning of 1967. (Gouache by Roger Chapelet).

COLOUR PLATES

I. MAJORCAN EMBROIDERESS AT PUERTO POLLENSA. Embroidery is probably one of the most widespread crafts in the Balearic Islands. There are actually schools in the villages where little girls from the age of six upwards learn the secrets of this delicate art; they make tablecloths, handkerchiefs and also fine lace, particularly the *rebozillo*, a cowl-like mantilla worn by the young girls when they put on their traditional costume on feast days. These children can often be seen in groups of ten around their teacher, laughing as they ply their needle in the round embroidery frame. Often their chairs are set in a row in the shady part of the street, against the wall of their 'school'. Thus a tradition contributing to the fame of the islands has been kept alive right up to the present day. *facing page 16*

II. NORIA ON THE ROAD TO POLLENSA. These bucket-chains, worked by a mule walking blindfold, are for drawing the water necessary to irrigate the fields. It is this sight which reminds tourists most forcibly how long the legacies of Moorish occupation have persisted. Often wind-pumps have replaced the norias; these are among the most characteristic features of the landscape around Palma, La Puebla and Muro. *facing page 32*

III. THE CLOISTER OF MIRAMAR. In 1276 Ramon Llull decided to build on this spot his school of oriental languages intended for the training of missionaries.

The buildings we see today are only about a quarter of those which existed in the thirteenth century. The cloister, which can be seen half-hidden among the luxuriant vegetation, is a fragment of a gallery brought from the convent of Santa Margarita in Palma at the end of the nineteenth century. The chapel, which is still in existence today, was originally part of the church which was there in Ramon Llull's time. *facing page 48*

IV. THE BEACH AT FORMENTOR. 'Eden was essentially a garden, and so, here too, there had to be a garden by the sea. . . . The bay is completely land-locked, and the sea lies in it as though in a cup, ringed by the mountains, beneath the great dome of the sky.' (R. Brasillach, *Comme le temps passe*). *facing page 64*

1. *Palma. Paseo Maritimo.*

Palma

2. *Es Jonquet.*

3. *Yachting Club Náutico.*

4. Palma.

5, 6. Palma.
La Lonja.

Palma
7. *Consulado del Mar.*
8. *La Almudaina.*

9. Palma. Paseo Sagrera.

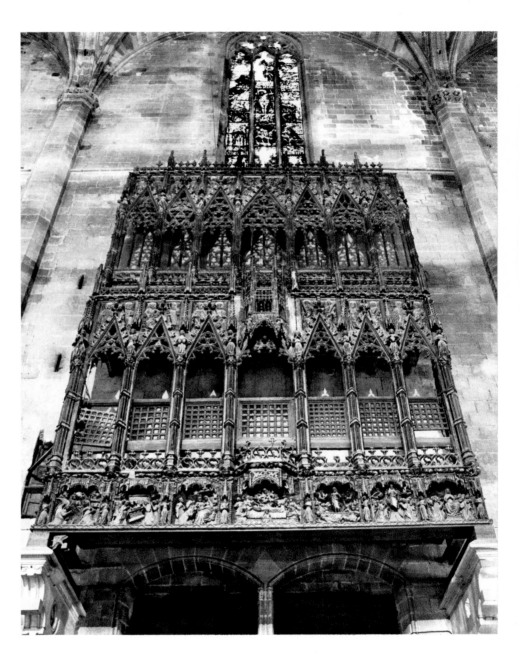

10, 11. Palma. La Seo.

12. *Palma.*

13, 14, 15. *Palma.*
Bellver.

16. Palma. San Francisco.

Palma
17. *San Francisco.*
18. *N. S. del Socorro.*

19. *Palma. Calle de
la Seo.*

20. *Palma.*

21. Palma. Calle de la Almudaina.

22. *Palma. Casa Oleza. Patio.*

23, 24. Palma. San Francisco.

Mallorca
25. Alfabia.
26. Raixa.

27. *Palma. Patio.*

28. Miramar.

29. Raixa.

30. *Valldemosa.*

31. *Valldemosa.*

32. *Valldemosa.*
Piano de Chopin.

33. Valldemosa.

34. *Paseo del Generalísimo (El Borne).*

35. *Andraitx.*

36. La Dragonera.

VILLA DE ANDRAITX
PALMA

37, 38. *Puerto de Andraitx.*

39. Mirador de Ricardo Roca.

40. *Mirador de Las Ánimas.*

41. *Coll de*
    Sa Gremola.

42. *Estellenchs.*

43. *La Foradada.*

44. *Puerto de Sóller.*

45. Sóll

46. Lluch.

47, 48. Buñola.

53. Ca'n Pilo.

49 à 52. Baix de Puig.

54. Miran

55. *La Puebla.*

56. Bañalbufar.

57. *Son Veri.*

58. *La Puebla.*   59. *La Puebla.*

60. *Calvario*
    de Pollensa.
61. *Selva.*

62. « Es Devellment ». Pollensa.

63. *Puerto de Pollensa.*

64. *Es Colomer.*

65. *Mirador*
  d'Es Colomer.

66. *Formentor.*

67, 68, 69. Alcudia.
Tarde de toros.

70. *Alcudia.*
71, 72. *Ca'n Picafort.*

73. *Puerto de Alcudia.*

74. *Pollensa.*

75. Artá.

76. *Capdepera.*
77. *Torre de Cañamel.*

78, 79, 80. Valldemosa.

81. Alcudia.

82, 83. *Campanet.*

84. *Porto Cristo.*

85. San Telmo.

86. *Ciudad Blanca (Alcudia).*

87. *Cala Figuera.*
88. *Porto Petro.*

89. Palma.

90. Puerto de Mahón.

91. Puerto de Mahón.

92. Puerto de Mahón.

93. Puerto de Mahón (XIXe).

94. *Cala Galdana.*

95. *Villa Carlos.*

96. San Luis.

97. San Luis.

98. *Fornells.*

99. *Taula y talayot de Trepuco.*

100. *Mercadal.*

101. *Naveta d'Es Tudons.*

102. *Puerto de Ciudadela.*

Ciudadela
103. El Borne.
104. El Rosario.

105. Ciudadela. Ses Voltes.

106. *Ciudadela.*

107. *Ibiza.*

108, 109, 110. Ibiza.

111. *Ibiza. Catedral.*

112. *Ibiza. Portal de Las Tablas.*

113. *San Jorge.*

114. *Ibiza. Calle de la Virgen.*

115. Ibiza. La Drassaneta.

116, 117. *Ibiza. Museo.*

118. *Santa Eulalia.*

119. San José.

120. San José.

121. Ibiza.

122. *Cala Portinatx.*

123. *San Antonio.*

124. *Santa Eulalia.*

125. *San Miguel.*

126. *Santa Eulalia.*

127. Ibiza.

128. *El Pilar.*

129. Formentera.

130. El Pilar. *131. Formentera.*

132. *Mola de Formentera.*

133. « Car Ferry ».